Homesteading Unplugged

An Ultimate Guide for a Sustainable Living in a Digital World

Table of Contents

Introduction

Fundamentally, homesteading is a way of life-based on sustainability, self-sufficiency, and a relationship with the land. Explore the world of homesteading through the vibrant pages of this book! I've delved deep into every facet of this lifestyle, offering a comprehensive guide that's perfect for newcomers seeking to forge their path towards a sustainable existence in our digital age.

Homesteading's historical foundations must be examined to be fully understood. The Homestead Acts of the late 19th and early 20th centuries in the United States are when the word "homesteading" first appeared. To promote westward migration, these acts were a piece of legislation that granted land to people who were prepared to settle on it and make it their own. In the once uncharted territory, homesteaders—often families or lone people with a spirit of adventure—claimed property and worked diligently to build houses, farms, and villages.

The tale of tenacity and will is the historical backdrop of homesteading. The difficulties encountered by homesteaders were seclusion, a hard environment, and few resources. Nevertheless, the enormous agricultural landscapes and towns that characterized the American frontier were developed due to their efforts.

Although the historical background sets the scene, homesteading in the present day takes many different forms. Nowadays, homesteading is practiced in suburban and even metropolitan areas rather than only on rural frontiers. It is the deliberate decision to live more sustainably, often shown by actions like keeping livestock, cultivating food, and reducing dependency on outside systems.

Individuals or families that aspire to a purposeful and thoughtful way of life are known as modern homesteaders.

They could adopt classic homesteading practices, like raising hens or gardening, while using cutting-edge inventions and technology to improve sustainability. This flexibility reflects how homesteading is changing in response to the possibilities and difficulties of the modern day.

There are several advantages to adopting a homesteading lifestyle that goes beyond personal or family benefits. The main benefit is that there is more self-sufficiency. Homesteaders contribute to a more robust way of life by producing their food, using renewable energy sources, and implementing sustainable methods that lessen their need on other organizations.

An additional primary advantage is environmental sustainability. As part of their active efforts to reduce their ecological impact, homesteaders often prioritize renewable energy sources, organic farming, and conservation techniques. This dedication to environmental stewardship aligns with global resource depletion and climate change worries.

Apart from its practical benefits, homesteading cultivates a deep feeling of community. Homesteaders often express a higher level of life pleasure, whether because of their relationship to the land, food, or community they establish. This satisfaction and purpose come from living a life that values simplicity, sincerity, and a closer relationship with nature.

Even while homesteading has many advantages, there are some hurdles, particularly in the twenty-first century. Zoning laws, economic demands, and the fast-paced digital world might hamper a more purposeful and sustainable style of living.

Economic factors, for example, can make starting a homestead financially unfeasible. It may take some time to see a return on initial expenditures made in land, equipment, and infrastructure. Because zoning laws are intended for people who live in traditional urban and suburban areas, they may limit some homesteading methods or set minimum requirements for the size of property parcels.

Developing the proper mentality and being dedicated to the homesteading adventure are the first steps toward overcoming these obstacles. The homesteader has an adaptable, resilient, and resourceful attitude. It entails the courage to try new things, learn, and commit to an ongoing development process.

A key component is commitment. A homestead involves a commitment to the ongoing responsibilities of tending to crops, taking care of animals, and maintaining sustainable systems. It requires a dedication to lifetime learning since homesteaders are always picking up new skills and adjusting to shifting conditions.

Homesteaders often implement digital detox techniques into their lives since they know the possible risks associated with digital reliance.

The digital world has permeated every aspect of our lives in the twenty-first century, changing how we work, communicate, and get information. Rapid technological advancement has made it possible to link individuals worldwide, streamline communication, and instantly access a wealth of knowledge, among other previously unimaginable comforts. But the digital revolution has also brought about a conflict with traditional living, especially for those who are turning to homesteading to live a more deliberate and sustainable existence.

Recognizing the significant influence of technology on a range of facets of our lives is essential to understanding the digital world. Digital communication, social media, online shopping, and smartphones have changed how we relate to one another, time, and location. The digital age is characterized by the rapidity with which information is exchanged and the ongoing connectedness that affects people's perceptions and interactions with their surroundings.

Homesteaders need a sophisticated view of technology to negotiate this conflict. They see technology critically even while they acknowledge its advantages, such as solar energy, environmentally friendly agricultural methods, and online learning tools. The homesteading way of life emphasizes striking a balance between connecting to traditional skills and traditions and using technology when needed.

Utilizing technology as a tool rather than becoming dependent on it is part of the deliberate use of technology in homesteading. For example, homesteaders may use the internet to reach other like-minded individuals, get instructional materials, or promote their eco-friendly goods. But as vital elements of their way of life, they also stress physical work, practical skills, and a close relationship with the earth.

Digital detoxification is setting aside time to perform physical labor, go outside, and connect with others in person instead of using digital gadgets. In addition to lessening the harmful impacts of continuous screen time, this practice supports the homesteading lifestyle's core principles of mindfulness and presence.

Homesteaders continue the long-standing custom of assisting one another by interacting in person, participating in community activities, and creating networks of mutual help. Intentionally working to fortify community links combats the isolating effects of digital reliance and helps build robust, linked local communities.

Fundamentally, the conflict between digital dependence and traditional life reflects a larger social contradiction. Instead of giving in to the potentially alienating effects of technology, homesteaders use it as a tool for sustainability. This allows them to handle this conflict with awareness and purpose.

Join the journey towards a sustainable lifestyle! Dive deeper into this book to uncover the wealth of insights waiting in the next chapters. Let's explore together and discover the keys to a greener, more mindful way of living. Continue the adventure now!

Purpose of the Book: Navigating Sustainable Living in a Digital Age

Amidst a society marked by rapid technological progress and a growing dependence on digital connection, the quest for sustainable living has become a countercultural movement that questions established conventions and ways of living. The idea for this book, "Homesteading Unplugged" came about when it became clear that the conflict between traditional living and digital reliance would greatly impact those looking for a more purposeful and sustainable way of life.

This book aims to provide a thorough introduction to homesteading in the digital era for individuals interested in taking the plunge or just starting out. It seeks to provide insightful analysis, useful suggestions, and a careful investigation of the connections between classic homesteading principles and the difficulties posed by our rapidly digitizing society.

Setting the Goal in Perspective:

Modern progress narratives favor convenience, digital connectedness, and technology developments. But during this story, more and more people are reassessing how they interact with technology and looking for alternatives that put sustainability, independence, and a closer connection with nature first. This book aims to tackle the special possibilities and problems brought about by this collision, providing a road map for those who want to successfully negotiate the intricacies of sustainable living in the digital era.

Guiding Concepts

Harmonizing Innovation with Tradition:

The book aims to balance cutting-edge, technologically-driven, sustainable living solutions and conventional homesteading methods. It recognizes that while certain technologies may improve the homesteading experience, a cautious approach is necessary to prevent falling prey to the dangers of being too reliant on technology.

Useful Tips for Living a Sustainable Lifestyle:

The book offers helpful advice for those who want to take up homesteading. Every chapter provides:

- Practical guidance based on sustainability principles.

- Covering topics such as selecting an appropriate site.

- Creating a sustainable homestead.

- Putting off-grid living strategies.

- Developing necessary homesteading skills.

Relationships and Community:

Understanding the value of community in the homesteading process, the book looks at how to create and maintain in-person relationships at a time when digital contacts predominate. It highlights the value of information sharing, resource sharing, and community support in building a strong and cohesive homesteading community.

Happiness and Mindfulness:

The book's main focus is on how homesteading lifestyles may include mindfulness techniques and a holistic approach to well-being. It looks at stress-reduction strategies, the therapeutic benefits of nature, and building a happy, balanced existence.

Managing an Ecological Lifestyle in the Digital Era:

The book's main goal is to help readers navigate the complex process of sustainable living while addressing the particular difficulties presented by the digital era. It answers queries like these:

- In a day where screens and gadgets rule the landscape, how can people stay connected to the land and the natural world?
- How can technology improve sustainability without undermining the core principles of traditional homesteading?
- What strategies do homesteaders use to reconcile the practicality of internet access with the deliberate, hands-on approach necessary for sustainable living?

In short, this book aims to enable people to pursue purposeful, resilient, and deeply rooted homesteading practices to live sustainably in the digital age. By negotiating the conflict between tradition and technology, readers may take a trip beyond the confines of traditional living and embrace a simple, real, and sustainable way of life. As we go through the remaining chapters, the book begins to take shape as a guide for those trying to figure out how to live sustainably in the digital age.

Chapter 1: The Homesteading Lifestyle

1.1 Historical Overview of Homesteading

To fully comprehend the homesteading way of life, one must go back to its historical origins, a story molded by the pioneering spirit of people pursuing self-reliance and freedom. The phrase "homesteading" conjures up images of the American frontier in the late 19th and early 20th centuries, when the Homestead Acts had a major influence.

The story of tenacity, grit, and the quest for a better life is the historical context of homesteading. The Homestead Acts passed in many stages between 1862 and 1934, allowed prospective settlers to claim portions of public property as long as they fulfilled certain requirements. Usually, these requirements included constructing a home, farming the land, and proving advancements over time. Homesteaders received land ownership in exchange, which encouraged the development of new settlements across the burgeoning American frontier.

Living off the Land on the Frontier:

Homesteading was a way of life on the frontier, not just a formal procedure. Families and individuals journeyed into the uncharted regions of the West, sometimes with nothing more than basic equipment and a strong will to succeed. They had to construct everything from the ground up, endure inclement weather, and overcome severe obstacles. Simple agricultural methods, cleared fields, and log huts became symbolic of the homesteading movement.

The frontier farmhouse was a symbol of hard labor and independence. It served as a laboratory for adaptation, where people created creative responses to the difficulties presented by an unfamiliar and sometimes harsh setting. In addition to claiming property, homesteading was a life-changing experience that shaped the identities of individuals who adopted this way of life.

Obstacles and Triumphs:

A summary of homesteading's past shows various struggles and successes. The prospect of free land drew in many, but the reality required much sacrifice and work. Homesteaders' grit was tested by the solitude of frontier life and the lack of contemporary conveniences. Nevertheless, many overcome these difficulties to establish prosperous settlements on the once undeveloped frontier by tenacity and group solidarity.

There was no one-size-fits-all experience with homesteading. The difficulties encountered by homesteaders varied according to geography, climate, and personal circumstances. Homesteaders modified their methods to fit the needs of their surroundings, whether they were in the West's mountainous regions or the Midwest's arid plains — this range of experiences enriched the rich fabric of homesteading history.

The Homestead Acts' Legacy:

In American history, the Homestead Acts' legacy lives on. The law made distributing more than 270 million acres of public property easier, drastically changing the country's geography and population. It supported agricultural growth and settlement, strengthening the country's social and economic foundation.

The legacy is complex, however. The influence of the Homestead Acts on indigenous inhabitants and the environment is still being considered despite its importance in the United States growth and the development of agricultural communities. The effects of westward expansion are multifaceted, including advantages and disadvantages that influenced the development of American history.

Homesteading Outside of the Border:

The idea of homesteading changed as the frontier age came to an end. The concept of homesteading endured even after the Homestead Acts' legal foundation was abandoned. Families and individuals maintained a way of life based on self-sufficiency and a relationship with the land, even as their environments changed from wild frontiers to populated areas.

Modern Homesteading:

The practice of homesteading has expanded throughout the modern era. It transcends historical geographic boundaries and may be found in suburban, rural, and even metropolitan environments. Modern homesteaders embrace the benefits and difficulties of the present while taking inspiration from the movement's historical foundations.

Anyone starting a homestead must thoroughly understand the practice's historical origins. It offers a basis, an inspiration source, and a reminder of the persistence of the human spirit, which longs for autonomy, self-reliance, and a link to the land. We shall follow the development of homesteading from its historical roots to its many manifestations in the modern day as we further examine the lifestyle.

1.2 Modern Interpretations and Adaptations

Although homesteading has its historical origins in the pioneer spirit of the American frontier, it has undergone substantial modern-day evolution. Modern interpretations and adaptations of the homesteading lifestyle result from the renewed interest in purposeful living, sustainability, and self-sufficiency in the twenty-first century.

Homesteading Outside of the Border:

Homesteading has greatly grown in the modern era, beyond the boundaries of the 19th century. It is becoming increasingly popular among people and families in various contexts, including suburban lots, rural acres, and even urban areas. It is centered on sustainability, self-sufficiency, and connection to the natural world. It is not only about how big the property is.

Taking Up Intentional Life:

Intentional living, which is the deliberate decision to create a lifestyle that aligns with one's own beliefs and environmental responsibilities, attracts modern homesteaders. This deliberate approach touches on many areas of everyday living, including energy and food use, waste minimization, and the overall influence on the environment. Today's Homesteaders want to reduce their environmental impact while developing a feeling of satisfaction and purpose.

Getting Used to Today's Challenges:

The difficulties that contemporary homesteaders experience are quite different from those of their frontier predecessors. Urbanization, zoning laws, and 21st-century economic realities present special challenges. However, modern homesteaders have an amazing capacity for adaptation, using technology, community support, and creative problem-solving to overcome these obstacles.

Technology Confusion:

Incorporating technology is one of the most significant changes in contemporary homesteading. While physical work and crude equipment were the hallmarks of historic homesteading, modern homesteaders often use technological improvements to increase efficiency and sustainability. Smart irrigation systems, solar panels, and online learning and community-building tools are a few examples of how technology may be used to enhance the homesteading way of life.

Urban and Suburban Agrarian Practices:

The modern homesteading movement has permeated suburban and urban environments. Urban homesteading means developing a self-sufficient way of life within urban boundaries, using little areas for gardening, keeping hens, and implementing sustainable methods. Despite having greater room, suburban homesteading often faces difficulties between zoning restrictions, the need to balance contemporary amenities, and a desire for independence.

Permaculture and Ecological Methods:

Contemporary homesteaders often adopt sustainable methods and permaculture concepts. The term "permanent culture" or "permanent agriculture" refers to a design concept called "permaculture," which aims to build sustainable and regenerative systems. Building robust and fruitful ecosystems entails imitating the connections and patterns seen in nature. Contemporary homesteaders incorporate permaculture into their gardening, farming, and general land management techniques.

Building Communities and Networks:

Modern homesteading is unique in its strong focus on networking and community development. While homesteaders in the past often suffered isolation, those in the present actively look for other like-minded people in their local and online groups. The contemporary homesteading movement's success and durability are attributed to cooperative efforts, pooled resources, and information sharing.

Access to Information and Education:

Another important change from historical homesteading is knowledge and educational resources availability. The benefit of contemporary homesteading is the availability of books, seminars, workshops, and internet resources on sustainable living methods. With so much knowledge, people may learn new skills, solve problems, and keep up with the most recent advancements in homesteading.

Harmonizing Innovation with Tradition:

Although homesteading today embraces creative solutions, it is firmly grounded in traditional values. The persistent values that unite historical and contemporary understandings of homesteading include the dedication to self-sufficiency, the production of one's food, and a relationship with the land. The trick is embracing the finest aspects of traditions and innovations while striking a harmonic balance between them.

In short, the homesteading lifestyle has been interpreted and modified in the modern day in response to the possibilities and problems of the modern world. People are reinventing what it means to live purposefully, sustainably, and with a strong connection to the environment on anything from rural landscapes to urban rooftops. We will examine how these contemporary interpretations materialize in the how-to's of designing a farm, putting sustainable practices into action, and building a sense of community in an increasingly digital society as we dive further into the next chapters.

1.3 Benefits of Embracing the Homesteading Lifestyle

With more people looking for alternatives to contemporary, fast-paced living, homesteading has gained popularity due to its many advantages. It is based on the ideas of sustainability, self-sufficiency, and a close relationship with the land, and has many benefits beyond benefits for the person or family. The many advantages of adopting a homesteading lifestyle in the modern world are examined in this section.

Flexibility and Self-Sufficiency:

The goal of independence and self-sufficiency is at the core of homesteading. Homesteaders lessen their need for outside systems by cultivating food, producing renewable energy, and implementing sustainable practices. Self-sufficient people feel empowered because they are in charge of vital areas of their existence, such as food production, energy use, and general well-being.

Sustainability of the Environment:

An important aspect of homesteading is environmental responsibility. Techniques like permaculture, organic agriculture, and conservation help to lessen the ecological footprint that people and families leave behind. Through adopting sustainable agricultural and living techniques and a deeper connection with the land, homesteaders play an active role in the preservation and regeneration of the ecosystem.

Relationship with Nature:

A significant advantage of homesteading is restoring one's connection to nature. In a world where digital displays and urban landscapes are taking over, homesteading provides a chance to reconnect with the natural world's rhythms. Living in peace with nature, working the land, and seeing seasonal changes cultivate a greater awareness of the natural world and a feeling of connection to the greater ecological system.

Food Quality and Health:

Homesteaders actively participate in growing their food, often using sustainable and organic agricultural methods. This hands-on method guarantees superior quality food without artificial chemicals and pesticides. Eating fresh food cultivated nearby improves one's general health and nutrition. Caring for a farm also involves physical activities that promote a healthy lifestyle and offer exercise.

Financial Savings:

Homesteading has significant long-term economic rewards, even if the initial outlay may need financial support. Growing one's food lowers grocery costs, while achieving energy independence with renewable resources may result in substantial utility bill savings. Homesteading fosters self-sufficiency, which may strengthen financial resilience and lessen reliance on other economic forces over time.

Adaptability in the Face of Unpredictability:

Homesteading helps people become more resilient by giving them the tools to deal with unpredictability. Growing food, making energy, and managing resources on one's own becomes very important in uncertain economic times when environmental issues arise or when supply chain interruptions occur. Homesteaders are more equipped with ingenuity and flexibility to handle unanticipated events.

Contentment and Gratitude:

A strong feeling of contentment and satisfaction is gained from the observable benefits of homesteading, such as a flourishing garden and a well-kept farm. Experiencing the tangible and intangible results of one's labor gives one a feeling of success and purpose. Homesteaders often express greater happiness because of the purposeful, practical labor required to maintain their way of life.

Collective and Common Ideas:

Like-minded people dedicated to sustainability, self-sufficiency, and a connection to the land are often drawn to the homesteading lifestyle. Creating and participating in a homesteading community offers a feeling of community, shared resources, and social support. The sharing of information, insights, and excess products improves ties within the community.

Possibilities for Education:

Learning to homestead is an ongoing effort. Homesteaders pursue lifelong learning through sustainable construction techniques, animal husbandry, or gardening. The way of living promotes experiential learning, curiosity, problem-solving abilities, and a growing comprehension of the interdependence of natural systems.

Customized and Purposeful Lifestyle:

People may create a lifestyle via homesteading consistent with their objectives and beliefs. A customized and deliberate way of life is made possible by homesteading, whether by selecting certain sustainable practices, cultivating a particular set of crops, or breeding animals for particular uses. This personalization adds to a feeling of authenticity and improves life quality overall.

Homesteading is a comprehensive style of living that appeals to those who want a more meaningful, sustainable way of life and a closer connection to the land. It encompasses everything from environmental sustainability to personal satisfaction and community development. We shall examine how these advantages materialize in the doable facets of homesteading—such as planning, off-grid living, sustainable agriculture, and community development—when we go further into the ensuing chapters.

Unique Benefits of Embracing the Homesteading Lifestyle

1. Self-Sufficiency and Independence: Homesteaders gain empowerment by growing their own food, generating renewable energy, and reducing reliance on external systems.

2. Environmental Sustainability: Homesteading practices, such as organic gardening and permaculture, contribute to reducing ecological footprints and preserving the environment.

3. Connection to Nature: Homesteading fosters a reconnection to nature, allowing individuals to immerse themselves in the natural world and live in harmony with the environment.

4. *Quality of Food and Health:* Homesteaders produce high-quality, organic food, contributing to better nutrition and overall health. Physical activity in homesteading also promotes a healthy lifestyle.5. Economic Savings: While initial investments are required, homesteaders experience long-term economic benefits through reduced grocery and utility bills, leading to financial resilience.

6. *Resilience in the Face of Uncertainty:* The skills acquired in homesteading make individuals more resilient in navigating economic instability, environmental challenges, and disruptions in the supply chain.

7. *Satisfaction and Fulfillment:* Tangible results, from a thriving garden to a well-maintained homestead, provide a deep sense of satisfaction and fulfillment.

8. *Community and Shared Values:* Homesteading communities offer social support, shared resources, and a sense of belonging for individuals with shared values.

9. *Educational Opportunities:* Homesteading involves continual learning, fostering hands-on education in gardening, animal husbandry, and sustainable building practices.

10. *Personalized and Intentional Living:* Homesteading allows for a personalized and intentional lifestyle aligned with individual values, enhancing overall quality of life.

1.4 Challenges Faced by Homesteaders Today

Although there are many advantages to the homesteading lifestyle, there are some challenges, especially in the modern day. Contemporary homesteaders traverse a terrain characterized by urbanization, zoning laws, and a swiftly changing climate. Anyone hoping to adopt the homesteading lifestyle in the modern day must recognize and overcome these obstacles.

1. Zoning laws and land accessibility:

Finding an appropriate property to homestead on might be quite difficult. Land availability has decreased due to urbanization, and zoning laws often determine how land is used in suburban and rural regions. There may be limitations on the kinds of buildings, livestock, and agricultural pursuits that homesteaders can engage in. While negotiating these restrictions, careful study, compliance with local laws, and sometimes advocating for more homesteader-friendly zoning ordinances are necessary.

2. A Look at the Economy:

Homesteading has long-term economic benefits, but it often necessitates upfront financial outlays. Acquiring land, building infrastructure, and investing in sustainable technology may be expensive. Homesteaders may have to work through financial difficulties to balance these initial costs to become self-sufficient in the long run. Additionally, outside variables like changes in supply costs and the availability of markets for items produced on homesteads may have an impact on the economic feasibility of homesteading.

3. Labor- and Time-Intensiveness:

Living on a homestead involves a lot of work and demands a significant time and energy commitment. Regular attention is required for off-grid system maintenance, animal care, and landscape maintenance. Homesteaders often have to juggle these duties with other commitments, including jobs and family duties. Finding a long-term solution to the demands of homesteading while juggling other responsibilities is a constant struggle.

4. The Learning Curve for Technology:

Although incorporating technology into homesteading may improve sustainability, a learning curve is involved. Using smart irrigation systems, renewable energy systems, and other technical solutions may require a degree of skill that homesteaders must acquire. It may be difficult to stay up to date with sustainable technology developments, so homesteaders need to make time for continuing education to get the most out of these resources.

5. Pressures from the Environment and Climate Change:

Modern homesteaders have an additional degree of complication due to the effects of climate change. The resilience of homesteads, including crops and cattle, may be jeopardized by harsh weather patterns, natural catastrophes, and unpredictable weather patterns. Strategic planning, resilience-building techniques, and a dedication to sustainable practices that lessen rather than exacerbate climate change are necessary for adapting to these environmental stresses.

6. Social and Community Difficulties:

Although homesteading groups might assist, contemporary homesteaders could have difficulties with acceptance and comprehension from the community. Not every community or neighborhood understands or is open to the homesteading way of life. Homesteaders may have societal obstacles that they must resolve amicably, such as misconceptions about their ability to support themselves, worries about the value of their land, or disputes with neighbors.

7. Obtaining Education and Resources:

From off-grid living and sustainable building to gardening and animal husbandry, homesteading requires a broad skill set. It might be difficult to get resources and educational opportunities, particularly for those living in rural or underdeveloped locations. Homesteaders must consult trustworthy sources for information on emerging technology, sustainable living trends, and best practices.

8. Juggling Homesteading and Work:

The difficulty of juggling regular work with the needs of homesteading is one that many contemporary homesteaders encounter. Because of the costs of maintaining a homestead, homesteaders sometimes have to labor off their property. To satisfy financial commitments and maintain the homesteading lifestyle, juggling these activities requires efficient time management.

9. Medical Care and Emergencies:

Homesteaders in isolated or rural locations could struggle for emergency services and healthcare. The distance from emergency services and medical facilities may influence the choice to choose a homesteading lifestyle. Making emergency plans and guaranteeing access to healthcare supplies become crucial for people or families that want to live in more remote homesteading areas.

10. Mental and Emotional Health:

The demands of self-sufficiency combined with the solitude that some homesteading lifestyles entail might hurt one's emotional and mental health. Stress or feelings of overload may be exacerbated by the responsibilities of running a farm, particularly under trying circumstances. A resilient homesteading lifestyle requires prioritizing mental health and developing a support system.

In summary, while homesteading provides a satisfying and sustainable way of life, it is critical to acknowledge and resolve the difficulties that contemporary homesteaders confront. Land accessibility, financial concerns, labor and time constraints, technology learning curves, social barriers, access to resources, work-life balance, healthcare issues, and emotional well-being are all included in this list of challenges. A resilient mentality, community involvement, ongoing learning, and strategic planning are all necessary to overcome these obstacles. In the next chapters, we'll delve into tactics, perspectives, and real-world examples illuminating how homesteaders surmount these obstacles and prosper in their quest for an intentional and sustainable way of life.

1.5 Setting the Foundation: Mindset and Commitment

To create the proper attitude and dedication, potential homesteaders must go through an inward journey before breaking ground, sowing crops, or rearing animals. Beyond mere practical expertise, a successful homesteading endeavor is based on a profound comprehension of the principles, frame of mind, and degree of dedication necessary to adopt a sustainable and self-sufficient way of life.

1. Fostering a Homesteading Mentality

A strong respect for simplicity is at the heart of the homesteading mentality. Homesteaders deliberately choose for a simple, low-consumption lifestyle that rejects excessive materialism. This way of thinking stresses the pleasure of the simple things in life, including taking care of the land, raising food, and coexisting with the natural world. It places a higher priority on quality than quantity.

Adaptability and Resilience:

By its very nature, homesteading entails adjusting to the unpredictable nature of the weather, the natural world, and the difficulties of sustainable living. It is crucial to have a resilient and adaptable attitude. Homesteaders understand that obstacles and disappointments are unavoidable and that success often requires a flexible approach to problem-solving and experience-based learning.

Long-Term Perspective and Patience:

Homesteading is a process rather than a final goal. Adopting this lifestyle requires people to have a long-term vision and develop patience. It takes time to establish a self-sufficient farm, and results may not show up immediately. The homesteading mentality recognizes the benefits of slow growth and the long-term gains from consistent work.

Ingenuity and Do-It-Yourself Mentality:

Homesteaders have a do-it-yourself (DIY) mentality and are resourceful people. People with a creative problem-solving approach aggressively seek answers within the available resources. A fundamental component of the homesteading mentality is resourcefulness, which may be used for everything from fixing a tool to constructing a structure to discovering new commodity applications.

2. Dedication to the Homesteading Way of Life:

Comprehending the Extent of Engagement:

Adopting a homesteading lifestyle requires a deep comprehension of the extent of the commitment. It covers more than just the idealized picture of a bucolic rural setting; it also includes the daily struggles, labor-intensive tasks, and accountability in running a sustainable farm. Potential homesteaders need to understand what lifestyle changes and commitments are involved.

Juggling Employment and Homesteading:

Homesteading often coexists with other obligations or formal jobs. Maintaining this lifestyle requires a careful balancing act between employment and homesteading responsibilities. Potential homesteaders must evaluate their ability to properly handle both facets and make well-informed choices on the scope and level of their homesteading endeavor.

Readiness for Finances:

To be a homesteader, one must be financially prepared. Long-term financial gains from homesteading are possible, but upfront expenses are related to purchasing property, setting up infrastructure, and investing in sustainable technologies. Prospective homesteaders should have a sensible budget and be aware of potential financial obstacles.

Taking the Family and Community Into Account:

Most of the time, homesteading is a family or communal project. People should consider their family or community members' willingness and excitement before committing. A common dedication to the homesteading way of life creates a nurturing atmosphere and enhances the whole experience.

Assessing Modifications to Lifestyle:

Adjusting to contemporary comforts and lifestyle standards is necessary while homesteading. Potential homesteaders need to be ready for a change in their priorities, how they spend their time, and how they use technology. A commitment to homesteading necessitates a readiness to adjust to a way of life that puts sustainability and self-sufficiency first.

3. Overcoming Obstacles and Remaining Dedicated:

Homesteading is often difficult; therefore, having a support network is crucial. Having a network of people to share experiences, ask for guidance, and provide support—whether they are family, friends, or other homesteaders—is essential for maintaining commitment in the face of difficulties.

Ongoing Education and Skill Advancement:

Maintaining a homesteading commitment requires a commitment to lifelong learning. People need to be proactive in learning new skills, keeping up with sustainable practices, and adjusting to changes in the homesteading environment.

Honoring Minor Triumphs:

It's important to recognize little wins, even during the daily grind. Acknowledging successes strengthens commitment and gives inspiration to keep going, whether it's cultivating a new crop successfully, resolving a technical issue, or seeing the benefits of sustainable practices.

Plans for Homesteading That Are Flexible:

Maintaining a homesteading commitment requires some planning flexibility. Unexpected difficulties can need modifying original plans. Long-term commitment requires the capacity to change course, evaluate, and adjust plans without losing sight of the main objective.

Fostering a Love of Homesteading:

Sustained dedication is propelled forward by passion. Homesteaders who develop a genuine affection for the way of life, the land, and the procedures involved are inspired to keep going. The perseverance required to overcome obstacles is fueled by passion, which also maintains the homesteading journey's sense of purpose and fulfillment.

In summary, developing the proper attitude and committing wholeheartedly to the lifestyle are essential to laying the groundwork for a successful homesteading endeavor. Appreciating resourcefulness, patience, resilience, simplicity, and a do-it-yourself attitude are all part of the homesteading mentality. Understanding the extent of the commitment, striking a balance between job and homesteading, being financially prepared, considering family and community needs, and being ready to make lifestyle changes are all necessary components of a homesteading lifestyle. Building a support network, learning new things constantly, acknowledging little accomplishments, being adaptable with your homesteading ideas, and developing a love for the homesteading lifestyle are all necessary for overcoming obstacles and remaining dedicated. Planning, sustainable agriculture, off-grid living, and community development are just a few of the practical components of homesteading that we will examine in more detail in the next chapters.

Chapter 2: Digital Disconnect

2.1 Understanding the Digital World

Understanding the intricacies of the digital world is essential to navigating the junction between traditional homesteading and the modern era. The term "digital world" refers to the broad terrain molded by online connection, digital technology, and the ubiquitous impact of the internet. This knowledge is fundamental for homesteaders looking to combine the advantages of digital technologies with the immersive, hands-on experiences of sustainable living.

1. The Digital Landscape's Evolution:

The way people connect, communicate, work, obtain information, and engage with society has changed dramatically due to the amazing expansion of the digital world. The digital world is always changing, from the introduction of personal computers to the widespread use of smartphones and high-speed internet. Gaining an understanding of this progression might help one appreciate the significant influence that digital technologies have on many facets of modern life.

2. Networking and Information Availability:

One of its distinguishing characteristics is the extraordinary interconnectedness that the digital world affords. The internet functions as a worldwide network, enabling immediate communication and offering access to vast data. The way people study, exchange information, and interact with a wide range of ideas has changed as a result of this connectedness. This connectedness provides homesteaders new chances for community development, online learning, and resource access that enhances conventional homesteading methods.

3. Electronic Resources and Tools for Homesteading:

Many tools and services in the internet realm are tailored to meet the demands of homesteading. Homesteaders worldwide are connected via websites, forums, and social media platforms, which facilitate sharing of information, advice, and experiences. Online markets make purchasing sustainable technology, equipment, and seeds easier. Homesteading YouTube channels, podcasts, and blogs provide insightful information. Homesteading may be improved by being aware of and using these digital tools well.

4. Online Shopping and Eco-Friendly Lifestyle:

Digital platforms significantly aid sustainable living. Homesteaders may choose environmentally friendly things with awareness thanks to e-commerce websites. A vast range of sustainable solutions are accessible via the internet economy, from acquiring off-grid equipment to locating organic seeds. Homesteaders are better able to match their values and purchases when they know how to use these platforms.

5. Issues with Reliance on Digital Media:

The digital era has many benefits, but it also brings with it drawbacks, especially when it comes to homesteading. Dependence on digital devices may cause one to lose touch with reality and the practical aspects of homesteading. The steady stream of information might lead to overload and take focus away from the homestead's urgent needs. For homesteaders looking to create a healthy balance, it is imperative that they comprehend the possible drawbacks of being too dependent on technology.

6. Effect on Equilibrium Work-Life:

The internet makes it difficult for those who combine regular jobs with homesteading to distinguish between work and personal life. Digital technologies make it easier to operate remotely, which may be flexible but can make it difficult to draw boundaries. Comprehending how internet connection affects work-life balance is crucial for homesteaders who want to balance their professional obligations and the requirements of sustainable living.

7. Using Social Media to Develop Communities:

Social media platforms effectively foster a sense of community among homesteading enthusiasts. Homesteaders may interact, exchange experiences, and assist Facebook groups, Instagram communities, and online forums. Knowing how to make the most of these platforms helps homesteaders connect with like-minded people worldwide and gives them a feeling of community.

8. Strategies for Digital Detox:

Homesteaders may put digital detox techniques into practice to mitigate the possible negative effects of continual digital contact. These deliberate pauses from screens and online activities promote mindfulness and a return to practical homesteading tasks by allowing for a connection with the natural world. A more balanced lifestyle is facilitated by realizing the benefits of digital detoxification and implementing it into daily homesteading activities.

9. Harmonizing Technology and Customs:

Conventional homesteading methods and the digital age don't have to conflict. One important thing to remember is striking a balance between technology and tradition. Online learning environments, weather monitoring applications, and smart irrigation systems may enhance conventional abilities without taking precedence over them. The trick is to use digital tools wisely to complement the practical components of homesteading rather than to replace them completely.

10. Security and Privacy Concerns:

Concerns about security and privacy are raised when homesteaders interact with the digital world. It is crucial to comprehend how to protect private data, secure online transactions, and operate digital platform privacy settings. Homesteaders may completely benefit from the digital world without jeopardizing their security by being aware of possible hazards.

In summary, managing sustainable living in the context of homesteading requires an awareness of the digital world. It entails appreciating how the digital world is changing, using digital tools and resources, tackling the problems associated with digital reliance, and striking a healthy balance between tradition and technology. Homesteaders who undertake this inquiry arm themselves to take advantage of the digital era's benefits while maintaining the core values of practical, sustainable living that define the homesteading way of life.

2.2 Impact of Digital Dependency on Sustainable Living

Given the growing integration of the digital world into everyday life, it is important to carefully analyze how digital dependence affects sustainable living, especially in the context of homesteading. Although digital technologies have many benefits, their widespread impact may threaten the core values of sustainable living—self-sufficiency, environmental responsibility, and active participation.

Environmental Footprint and Energy Use:

Digital gadgets and the infrastructure that supports the digital world greatly impact energy consumption and the environment. Carbon emissions and resource depletion are associated with electronic gadgets' production, use, and disposal. Homesteaders must consider the environmental effects of their digital activities and look for solutions to lessen them to live a sustainable lifestyle. This entails carefully selecting equipment for their kind and longevity and implementing energy-saving solutions.

Management of E-Waste:

Electronic garbage, or "e-waste," is becoming a bigger problem due to the quick turnover of electronic gadgets. Because they contain potentially dangerous elements, disposing of old or broken electronics may hurt the environment. Sustainable living ideas strongly emphasize waste management, encouraging homesteaders to look into possibilities for recycling, reusing, or appropriately disposing of technological equipment. Resolving the e-waste issue is crucial to coordinating digital use with environmentally friendly activities.

Diversion from Interactive Tasks:

Focusing on digital dependence may divert attention from practical tasks essential to a healthy lifestyle. Homesteaders may get disoriented from their immediate responsibilities, such as tending to crops, taking care of animals, and maintaining off-grid systems if they are constantly connected to digital devices, receiving alerts, and engaging in online activities. A crucial factor to consider is finding a balance that permits the advantages of digital technologies without compromising the immersive nature of practical homesteading.

Lessening of Direct Physical Contact:

Living sustainably requires having a tangible and direct relationship with the environment. If left unchecked, digital reliance might result in less time spent physically connecting with the land. The ease with which automated systems, remote communication, and internet research may be used may reduce time spent outside and the tactile sensations vital to sustainable practices. Homesteaders who use digital technologies to increase efficiency must be careful to maintain the physicality that is part of sustainable life.

Reliance Too Much on Technology-Based Solutions:

From smart irrigation systems to weather monitoring applications, digital technologies provide homesteaders with answers to various problems. However, relying too much on technology might cause one to lose touch with conventional knowledge and methods. Sustainable living promotes an all-encompassing strategy that balances traditional knowledge preservation and technological integration. Maintaining a balance between digital and conventional techniques guarantees a thorough and durable approach to homesteading.

Effect on Community and Social Dynamics:

The digital world makes Online communities and relationships easier, yet too much digital interaction might hurt local social dynamics. Shared resources and community collaboration are typically key components of sustainable living. A decrease in in-person encounters might result from digital reliance, which could impede the growth of robust local networks. For a more resilient and encouraging homesteading experience, homesteaders must be aware of striking a balance between developing in-person community interactions and digital connectedness.

Online shopping and consumerism:

Even in the case of sustainable living, the accessibility of internet buying might reinforce a consumerist mentality. Although eco-friendly items are available on digital platforms, the ease of internet shopping might encourage excessive consumption and hasty purchases. Homesteaders must exercise judgment while navigating the digital economy and make sustainable, purposeful decisions supporting mindful consumerism and self-sufficiency.

Data Security and Privacy Issues:

Dependence on digital platforms brings up significant issues with data security and privacy. Data sharing is required for integrating smart technology, including internet platforms and automated systems, into homesteading. Homesteaders must exercise caution when comprehending and handling the privacy consequences of their online activity. By putting strong security measures in place, digital technologies can improve household security rather than undermine it.

Possibility of Technological Discontinuity:

The possibility of technical obsolescence is brought about by the quick speed at which technology develops. Homesteaders' systems and equipment might become antiquated, making replacement, maintenance, and repair more difficult. Living sustainably promotes long-lasting and robust solutions. To prevent needless waste and resource consumption, homesteaders must carefully consider the durability and sustainability of digital technology incorporated into their operations.

Juggling Sustainability and Convenience:

Digital products often make time-saving, effective, and convenient promises. However, it takes judgment to balance these comforts and sustainable living methods. Homesteaders must evaluate whether digital solutions bring unexpected implications or align with sustainability ideals. Maintaining a balance between environmental responsibility and efficiency guarantees a comprehensive strategy for incorporating digital technologies into the homesteading way of life.

To put it briefly, the effects of digital dependency on sustainable living in the context of homesteading entail navigating issues with energy use, managing e-waste, getting distracted from practical tasks, reducing physical engagement, relying too much on technological solutions, influencing social dynamics, consumerism, potential technological obsolescence, and striking a careful balance between convenience and sustainability. Maintaining the integrity of the homesteading lifestyle becomes more dependent on conscientious decision-making and a dedication to sustainable practices as homesteaders navigate the digital age.

2.3 The Homesteading Perspective on Technology

The homesteading viewpoint on technology is a compass in the complex tango between traditional homesteading and the digital era. Homesteaders recognize technology's advantages and disadvantages while navigating this juncture with sophisticated knowledge to achieve sustainable living. This viewpoint is based on a dedication to environmental conservation, self-sufficiency, and a well-rounded strategy that balances digital technologies' advantages with homesteading's practical values.

Technology: Not a Master, Just a Tool:

Homesteaders see technology as an adjunct to their methods, not a means of replacing them. Digital technologies collect data, organize work, and increase productivity. The homesteading viewpoint does, however, maintain an important distinction: technology works for the homesteader, not the other way around. This way of thinking ensures that technology utilization aligns with the main objectives of self-sufficiency and sustainability.

Improving Conventional Knowledge:

Integrating technology might improve traditional homesteading abilities rather than replace them. For instance, automated systems may aid resource management, and weather-tracking applications can supplement traditional approaches to weather pattern prediction. Homesteaders use technology to enhance their skills and knowledge because they understand that combining contemporary tools with traditional knowledge creates a more robust homesteading practice.

Eco-friendly Technology:

The use of sustainable technologies is given priority in the homesteading stance on technology. Eco-friendly agricultural equipment and renewable energy sources are among the alternatives that homesteaders look for to support their environmental responsibilities. Selecting long-lasting, low-impact technology on the environment and low-energy-consuming is consistent with the homesteading philosophy of sustainable living.

Conscientious Use of Digital Resources:

When using internet tools, homesteaders use awareness. The viewpoint prioritizes quality over quantity and encourages the purposeful use of digital technologies that improve the homesteading experience in concrete ways. Homesteaders weigh the needs and effects of each digital resource, making decisions consistent with sustainability, as opposed to giving in to the newest devices or fashions.

Do It Yourself Tech Approach:

The do-it-yourself (DIY) attitude toward technology is a part of the homesteading culture. Homesteaders tend to have a hands-on approach to technology, even if they acknowledge the benefits of certain digital technologies. Homesteaders may better grasp their tools by creating, fixing, or altering digital solutions, which promotes self-sufficiency in both the physical and digital domains.

Adopting Low-Tech Remedies:

Low-tech and no-tech solutions are valued from the homesteading standpoint. Not every problem can be solved with technology. Homesteaders like the grace of straightforward, manual solutions that complement sustainable methods. When low-tech alternatives work well and fit into the homesteading lifestyle, the homesteading viewpoint accepts them, whether they be hand tools for gardening or traditional preservation techniques.

Using Technology for Networking and Education:

Homesteaders use technology for community networking and education. Social media, online forums, and online platforms link homesteaders worldwide, creating a support and knowledge-sharing network. New and experienced homesteaders may benefit from the instructional materials, tutorials, and professional guidance via digital resources.

Maintaining a Balance with Nature:

A fundamental aspect of the homesteading approach to technology is striking a balance between digital connections and a connection to the natural world. Homesteaders understand the value of disconnecting from technology and spending time in the real world, even if internet information and communication tools are also useful. Instead of acting as a barrier, technology links to the organic rhythms of rural life.

Using Technological Diversity to Build Resilience:

Homesteaders welcome technological variety as a resiliency tactic. Homesteaders understand the need for redundancy and variety in their technical toolset and don't depend only on high-tech solutions. By reducing the likelihood of technical malfunctions, this strategy ensures the homestead can continue operating and be sustainable even in the face of difficulties.

Ongoing Education and Adjustment:

The homesteading viewpoint is flexible and dynamic when it comes to technology. Homesteaders are aware that technology changes constantly and that knowledge is power. Homesteaders can make well-informed judgments and modify their approach to technology according to their developing sustainability knowledge via constant learning about new technologies, updates, and best practices.

To sum up, the homesteading viewpoint on technology is a thoughtful and sophisticated strategy incorporating electronic devices within a sustainable living philosophy. Homesteaders see technology as a tool, value its contribution to the development of traditional skills, select sustainable technologies, practice mindful consumption, take an interest in do-it-yourself projects, value low-tech solutions, use technology to network and for education, strike a balance between technology and nature, welcome technological diversity for Resilience, and uphold a commitment to lifelong learning and adaptation. This viewpoint guarantees that technology functions as a useful friend in the quest for self-sufficient and sustainable homesteading methods, enhancing the experience without undermining its core values.

Homesteading Perspective on Technology

1. Technology as a Tool, Not a Master: Homesteaders view technology as a tool to enhance, rather than dominate, their practices.

2. Enhancing Traditional Skills: Integration of technology is seen as a means to enhance, not replace, traditional homesteading skills.

3. Sustainable Technologies: The perspective prioritizes the adoption of sustainable technologies aligned with environmental responsibility.

4. Mindful Consumption of Digital Resources: Homesteaders exercise mindfulness in consuming digital tools, prioritizing quality over quantity.

5. DIY Approach to Technology: A hands-on mentality extends to technology, with homesteaders embracing a DIY approach.

6. Embracing Low-Tech Solutions: Acknowledges the value of low-tech and no-tech solutions, appreciating simplicity.

7. Technology in Education and Networking: Leverages technology for education, connecting homesteaders globally through online platforms.

8. Balancing Connectivity with Nature: Maintains a balance between digital connectivity and connection to the natural environment.

9. Resilience Through Technological Diversity: Values technological diversity for resilience, avoiding sole reliance on high-tech solutions.

10. Continuous Learning and Adaptation: Recognizes the dynamic nature of technology, prioritizing continuous learning and adaptation.

2.4 Finding Balance: Digital Detox Strategies

In the ever-expanding digital era, when screens are present in every aspect of contemporary life, striking a balance between the practicality of technology and the earthy, humbling homesteading traditions becomes crucial. In the context of homesteading, digital detox tactics are a purposeful and mindful attempt to recover moments of undistracted presence, promoting a peaceful coexistence between the digital and the analog.

Understanding the Requirement for Digital Detox:

Acknowledging the need for digital detoxification is the first step towards homesteading. Homesteaders recognize the possible drawbacks of continual internet interaction as they set out on a path rooted in sustainability and self-sufficiency. Homesteaders recognize the need to take occasional breaks from technology for their mental health and a stronger connection with their homestead, despite the appeal of social media, the never-ending barrage of alerts, or the desire to lose themselves in virtual worlds.

Creating Technology Breaks with a Purpose:

Instead of seeing digital detox as an arbitrary constraint, homesteaders view it as a deliberate discipline. Their tech breaks are planned to fit the cadence of their homesteading tasks. Conscientious preparation guarantees that the digital detox becomes an essential element of the homesteading routine, whether a weekly day of total digital disconnection or set aside hours for concentrated, tech-free labor on the property.

Establishing Digitally-Free Areas:

The homestead's physical surroundings greatly influence digital detoxification. Some regions are designated as "digital-free zones" by homesteaders. These spaces — be they social meeting places, reading nooks, or gardens—act as havens away from the distractions of technology. Homesteaders may completely immerse themselves in the sensory sensations of their environment without being interrupted by devices by creating these purposeful places.

Taking Part in Analog Exercises:

During times of digital detoxification, analog activities become more important. Homesteaders rediscover the pleasure of analog activities, such as reading books on paper, doing crafts by hand, or just taking peaceful time to observe the natural environment. Engaging in analog activities offers homesteaders a break from screen time while reintroducing them to the concrete and tactile elements of sustainable living.

Adopting Techniques for Mindfulness:

In homesteading, digital detox goes beyond just giving up devices; it also includes mindfulness exercises. Homesteaders incorporate moments of mindfulness into their daily routine via various means, such as taking deliberate breaths, strolling mindfully about the property, or meditating in a peaceful area. Keeping kids rooted in the here and now, these activities help students feel more connected to the land and the tasks.

Delineating Limits for Digital Devices:

A key component of digital detoxification is establishing limits with digital gadgets. Homesteaders set aside certain hours to check their social media accounts, emails, and other internet activity. This deliberate strategy ensures that internet connections don't interfere with everyday living or infringe on the necessary chores of homesteading.

Giving Face-to-Face Conversations Priority:

Homesteaders cherish in-person relationships and prioritize them while undergoing digital detoxification. The homesteading community is strengthened by promoting face-to-face contact via group dinners, cooperative projects, or nights around a campfire. Making in-person connections a priority helps homesteaders feel supported and like they belong.

Including Frequent Time Outs for Nature:

The strongest remedy for digital overload is nature. Whether it's a quick stroll, some stargazing, or just pausing to take in the sounds of the surroundings, homesteaders make frequent trips into the great outdoors part of their daily schedule. Homesteaders may refuel, refocus, and take in the surrounding natural beauty during these pauses.

Applying Digital Simplicity:

A key component of homesteading's digital detox is digital minimalism, the deliberate removal of digital distractions and clutter. To build a digital environment that is in keeping with their objectives and beliefs, homesteaders simplify online interactions, tidy digital places, and delete pointless programs.

Considering and Assessing Impact:

In homesteading, digital detoxification is developing and calls for consideration and assessment. Homesteaders regularly evaluate digital detox's effects on their general contentment, productivity, and well-being. This introspective method enables tweaks and improvements to guarantee that the digital detox stays a beneficial and long-lasting part of the homesteading way of life.

In summary, achieving equilibrium via digital detox techniques is essential to balancing the traditional and digital spheres in homesteading. Important elements of this deliberate approach include:

- We are acknowledging the need for detoxification.

- We are planning intentional breaks.

- We are establishing digital-free zones.

- I am participating in analog activities.

- We are adopting mindfulness practices.

- We are establishing boundaries with digital devices.

- We are giving priority to in-person interactions.

- Incorporating nature breaks.

- I am practicing digital minimalism.

- I am considering the effects.

Homesteaders may recapture moments of the present, foster a closer connection with the land, and develop a sustainable and conscientious way of living in the digital era by incorporating digital detoxification into their lifestyle.

2.5 Cultivating Real-world Connections in a Digital Era

Building in-person relationships is a transforming and essential undertaking in this age of internet connectedness, particularly in homesteading. Homesteaders must strike a delicate balance between modern technology's benefits and in-person interactions' deep value. Cultivating real-world connections is essential to strengthening communities, promoting knowledge sharing, and maintaining the core values of the homesteading way of life.

Making in-person relationships a priority:

Making in-person contacts a priority on purpose is essential to building real-world ties. Homesteaders intentionally work to cultivate deep relationships with neighbors, other homesteaders, and local community members because they understand the inherent significance of face-to-face contact. These ties go beyond the digital sphere, forming connections based on mutual trust, common experiences, and unity.

Community Events and Workshops:

Community workshops and get-togethers are dynamic channels for fostering relationships in the real world. Homesteaders plan and participate in gatherings, encouraging people to collaborate on projects, trade skills, and share information. These get-togethers, which can include workshops on sustainable farming methods, group barn-raisings, or seed exchanges, provide chances for in-person conversations that strengthen the bonds within the homesteading community.

Barter systems and shared resources:

Building relationships in the real world requires the homesteading group to build systems of barter and shared resources. Homesteaders understand that being self-sufficient doesn't equate to being alone but fosters cooperation. Mutual help is encouraged when resources, tools, and equipment are shared. Homesteaders who participate in barter systems, where they trade products and services, strengthen their bonds by fostering a feeling of reciprocity and dependency.

Trade and Local Farmers' Markets:

Homesteaders are further integrated into the community by participating in local farmers' markets and trading. Homesteaders directly contact neighbors and consumers and support the local economy by selling their vegetables, handcrafted crafts, or artisanal products. These in-person interactions promote a feeling of belonging to the community and respect for the work done by other homesteaders.

Collaboration and Support in the Neighborhood:

In the digital age, developing real-world relationships becomes contingent upon local collaboration and support. Homesteaders build strong support networks by interacting with their nearby neighbors and lending a hand when required. These acts of neighborly generosity, whether offering assistance during hectic seasons or sharing extra harvests, create relationships beyond screens.

Forming Cooperatives for Homesteading:

Cooperatives for homesteading are cooperative endeavors in which homesteaders combine effort, resources, and expertise to accomplish common objectives. These collaborative endeavors extend beyond virtual communications; they include in-person brainstorming sessions, team projects, and frequent gatherings. Initiating homesteading cooperatives fosters community members' feelings of shared responsibility and solidarity while also improving self-sufficiency.

Taking Part in Regional Community Projects:

Homesteaders actively participating in local community activities align with larger attempts to improve communal well-being. Homesteaders play a crucial role in the general well-being of the neighborhood by becoming involved in community garden projects, environmental conservation efforts, and educational activities. These in-person relationships develop ties throughout the community and go beyond digital divides.

In-person instruction and skill exchange:

Homesteaders understand the special benefits of in-person instruction and skill-sharing despite the abundant material available on digital platforms. Homesteading novices might benefit from direct mentoring and the sharing of information from seasoned homesteaders via workshops, apprenticeships, and practical training sessions. In addition to developing skills, these in-person encounters create enduring bonds between people with a similar enthusiasm for sustainable living.

Using Common Spaces to Build Communities:

Establishing communal areas within the homesteading community promotes impromptu conversations and get-togethers. These areas, which may be anything from a shared office to a dedicated gathering place to a common garden, serve as hubs for in-person interactions. To create a feeling of community and belonging, homesteaders congregate in these places to share experiences, exchange ideas, and work together on projects.

Accepting Social and Cultural Events:

Building real-world relationships is more than just the pragmatic side of homesteading; it also entails supporting social and cultural gatherings that honor the community's diversity. Homesteaders use festivals, potlucks, and seasonal festivities as opportunities to gather together, exchange customs, and deepen their sense of community. These gatherings provide chances for sincere relationships beyond everyday internet exchanges.

In conclusion, building genuine relationships in the digital age among homesteaders is a complex and deliberate endeavor. It entails putting face-to-face interactions first, planning community events and workshops, setting up shared resources and barter systems, participating in neighborhood cooperation, forming homesteading co-ops, participating in local community initiatives, encouraging in-person learning and skill-sharing, establishing common spaces, and welcoming social and cultural events. People who include these activities in their homesteading lifestyle establish connections that transcend the digital sphere, building a strong and cohesive community based on common principles and a dedication to sustainable living.

Chapter 3: Planning Your Homestead

3.1 Choosing the Right Location

Choosing the appropriate site is one of the most important decisions in starting a homestead. The selected location's geographical and environmental features significantly influence homesteading initiatives' effectiveness and sustainability. Selecting the ideal site requires careful consideration of factors such as climate and resource availability and compatibility with the homesteader's vision and aspirations for sustainable living.

Considering the Climate:

The climate is one of the main considerations when choosing a site for a homestead. The kinds of crops that can be grown, the animals that can be kept, and the general way of life that a homesteader might anticipate are all determined by the climate. Planning and modifying sustainable activities requires understanding seasonal fluctuations, temperature ranges, and precipitation patterns. Homesteaders have two options: they may focus on homesteading techniques suited to certain climates, such as dry or cold areas, or they can settle in areas with moderate conditions that sustain a wide variety of flora and animals.

Soil composition and quality:

The basis for sustainable agriculture is the soil on a farmhouse. Evaluating the composition and condition of the soil is crucial for productive land overall and for effective crop development. Homesteaders assess variables, including nutrient content, drainage, and soil texture. Determining the distinct qualities of the soil in the selected area and conducting soil tests can guide judgments on crop selection, fertilization plans, and sustainable land management techniques.

Obtaining Water Resources Access:

Selecting the ideal homestead site requires access to consistent water supplies. Water availability is essential for sustainable life, whether from underground aquifers, natural water sources like rivers and lakes, or precipitation patterns. Homesteaders evaluate the availability and quality of water supplies, devise plans for effective irrigation techniques, and consider ways to gather and conserve water. The homestead's resilience is ensured via sustainable water management, especially in light of shifting climatic trends.

Biodiversity and the Health of Ecosystems:

A homestead's capacity to survive over the long run is greatly influenced by the condition of the surrounding environment and the amount of biodiversity. Pollination, natural pest management, and ecological balance are all aided by a healthy ecology. Homesteaders look for areas with resilient ecosystems and conserved biodiversity. The objective of improving biodiversity and preserving a sound ecological balance on the farm is in line with the integration of permaculture principles, which emphasize working with natural systems.

Zoning and Legal Considerations

Selecting the ideal site for a homestead requires careful consideration of legal and zoning issues. Homesteaders must overcome zoning rules, municipal ordinances, and land-use limitations that may limit their capacity to carry out certain tasks. Adherence to legal mandates guarantees a seamless and enduring experience of homesteading.

Homesteaders have two options: they may participate in advocacy campaigns to influence laws that encourage sustainable living, or they can choose areas with zoning that permit agricultural methods.

Convenience to Vital Services:

Self-sufficiency is often the aim of homesteading, yet accessibility to necessary services is necessary for practical reasons. Selecting the ideal site requires consideration of accessibility to emergency services, medical facilities, and educational institutions. By balancing easy access to essential services and rural isolation, homesteaders ensure their way of life is sustainable and supported by the larger community infrastructure.

Renewable Resources and Energy Efficiency:

When choosing a site, homesteaders who are dedicated to sustainable living often give top priority to renewable resources and energy efficiency. Assessments of the availability of sunshine for solar energy, wind patterns for wind energy, and other renewable resources influence decisions on off-grid living and sustainable energy solutions. Selecting a site that offers ideal circumstances for using renewable energy is consistent with the values of reducing environmental effects and encouraging self-reliance.

Dynamics of Culture and Community:

The local community and culture greatly influence the experience of homesteading. Homesteaders can look for places with thriving local communities, supportive culture, and comparable ideals. Sustainable living includes:

- She was interacting with regional customs.

- I am taking part in community activities.

- We are enhancing the area's cultural landscape.

Homesteaders and their neighbors benefit from resilience and mutual support fostered by a feeling of community.

Economic Prospects and Difficulties:

Homesteaders take into account the geographical and economic potential of a certain area. This entails evaluating the employment market, the local economy, and the possibility of generating revenue using sustainable techniques. The location's economic viability influences the homesteader's capacity to attain self-sufficiency and financial sustainability. While some homesteaders concentrate on enhancing economic resilience via local, sustainable projects, others could choose areas with burgeoning local markets for their crops.

Climate Change Resilience:

In a time of climate change, homesteaders consider a location's ability to withstand obstacles connected to climate change. This entails assessing the vulnerability to severe weather, changes in precipitation patterns, and several climate-related variables. In response to climate change, homesteaders employ adaptive strategies, including drought-tolerant crops, water-saving techniques, and climate-resilient infrastructure, to secure the homestead's long-term sustainability.

In summary, the selection of an appropriate site for a homestead is a complex and strategic process that takes into account a variety of factors, including the climate, soil and water quality, biodiversity, legal and zoning issues, accessibility to necessary services, energy efficiency, cultural and community dynamics, economic prospects, and climate change resilience. The approach requires a comprehensive comprehension of the land and its environs, ensuring that the homesteader's vision is in harmony with the local natural and cultural features. Homesteaders build a resilient and sustainable lifestyle that aligns with their goals and beliefs by giving these aspects great thought.

3.2 Assessing Resources and Climate

An essential first step in starting a homestead is evaluating the climate and available resources. The complex interplay of local climate and natural resource availability greatly influences homesteaders' opportunities and difficulties as they strive for sustainable living. A detailed grasp of these variables, which range from soil fertility to sunshine and rainfall patterns, guides judgments about crop selection, land management, and the general layout of a resilient and sustainable farm.

Fertility and Composition of Soil:

The tale of sustainable living is portrayed on the soil that a farmhouse is constructed on. Since soil fertility and composition directly impact agricultural effort performance, evaluating them is an essential part of planning. Homesteaders analyze their soil to ascertain crucial elements like pH levels, nutrient content, and soil structure. Decisions on crop selection, fertilization techniques, and sustainable land management methods are guided by this knowledge.

Recognizing the complex network of fungi, organic matter, and microbes that support a robust and healthy soil ecosystem is essential to understanding soil fertility. By using techniques like composting, rotating planting, and covering crops, homesteaders aim to improve soil fertility. The foundation of sustainable agriculture is this proactive approach to soil health, which promotes long-term resilience and production.

Environmental Aspects

A homestead's sustainability and viability are determined by its climate. To customize their methods to the particular circumstances of their selected site, homesteaders examine a variety of meteorological variables. Temperature ranges, precipitation patterns, and seasonal fluctuations greatly influence the potential for agricultural, livestock management, and general homesteading activities.

Comprehending the microclimates present in the selected area yields sophisticated perspectives. There's a chance that certain parts of the homestead get more sunshine, have better airflow, or are more protected from the main winds. These microclimatic factors influence the homestead's general architecture, the placement of buildings, and planting places.

Water Management and Availability:

An essential component of sustainable homesteading is having access to water resources. Understanding the number and quality of water sources on or near the homestead is necessary to assess water availability. Homesteaders assess the dependability of water sources by considering variables, including rainfall patterns, the existence of natural water bodies, and the possibility of underground aquifers.

Sustainable living requires water management measures, especially when water shortage is an issue. Homesteaders use drip irrigation, rainwater collection, and water-conserving landscaping to maximize water consumption. In addition to providing for urgent water demands, the objective is to develop a robust water management system resistant to precipitation and climate variations.

Factors Associated with Sunlight and Microclimate:

The main factor influencing plant growth and total household production is sunlight. Mapping the homestead's daily and seasonal patterns of sunshine exposure is necessary to evaluate the amount of sunlight available. Homesteaders locate the best spots for solar energy systems, fruit orchards, and vegetable gardens in terms of sunshine exposure.

The evaluation of sunlight and climate is made more difficult by taking microclimate factors into account. Some parts of the homestead may be more or less vulnerable to wind, cold, or extreme heat. Homesteaders may deliberately design the location of buildings, windbreaks, and sensitive crops to enhance production and reduce susceptibility to severe weather events by understanding these microclimatic variations.

Wind Directions and Shelter Design:

When designing a resilient and sustainable homestead, it is essential to understand the local wind patterns. Homesteaders evaluate possible wind exposure regions, wind velocity, and prevailing winds. This knowledge informs decisions about positioning windbreaks, buildings, and delicate crops. Careful placement may prevent soil erosion, lessen plant stress, and improve household comfort and safety in general.

Homesteaders may create protected spaces by designing landscapes with natural windbreaks like hedgerows or tree lines. Alternatively, they can use buildings or fences to create artificial windbreaks. Homesteaders help to create microclimates that promote the health of both plants and animals by adjusting to the local wind patterns.

Natural Resources and the Health of Ecosystems:

Sustainable homesteading requires evaluating the area's natural resources and the general state of its ecosystem. Homesteaders identify local plant species, animal habitats, and ecological processes to better understand the region's biodiversity. This understanding informs practices for land management that support ecological balance and conservation.

Through the use of permaculture principles—which stress emulating natural ecosystems—homesteaders actively contribute to the health of ecosystems. Homesteaders increase biodiversity and strengthen the resilience of the regional environment by using strategies including companion planting, agroforestry, and habitat protection. These methods aid in the development of a regenerative and self-sufficient farmstead.

Diversity of Microbes and Ecosystem:

The soil's microbial and biological variety are essential to a healthy homestead environment. Homesteaders learn about the symbiotic ties between plants and soil microorganisms by delving into the tiny realm of soil biology. One way to measure microbial diversity is to examine the existence of good bacteria, fungi, and other microorganisms that support soil health and nutrient cycling.

Homesteaders use techniques like cover crops, low tillage, and adding organic matter to promote microbial diversity. These methods improve the general microbial activity, nutrient availability, and soil structure. Consequently, the soil ecosystem becomes robust and rich, supporting the development of healthy plants and enhancing the homestead's overall sustainability.

Geological Characteristics and Landform Issues:

The landforms and geological features influence the homestead's physical attributes. Slope, height, and the existence of geological formations are among the variables that homesteaders evaluate. Decisions on the location of buildings, water management techniques, and the general design of the homestead are influenced by this knowledge.

Comprehending the land's geological characteristics is especially important when dealing with possible obstacles like soil erosion on hills or rocky terrain. To lessen the influence of the land's geological characteristics, homesteaders may use erosion control techniques such as terrace systems, contour plowing, and other techniques.

Risk Evaluation and Adaptation Techniques:

A thorough risk assessment is required when evaluating the climate and available resources. Homesteaders recognize possible hazards, including severe weather, a lack of water, or deteriorating soil. The creation of adaptation measures to reduce risks and improve the homestead's overall resilience is made possible by this proactive approach.

Crop diversification to tolerate varying climatic conditions, water-saving technology, and agroecological techniques to improve soil resilience are a few examples of adaptation measures. Homesteaders position themselves to handle uncertainty and maintain their homesteading practices throughout time by foreseeing and preparing for probable obstacles.

Sustainability and Long-Term Vision Objectives:

The homesteader's long-term vision and sustainability objectives are inextricably tied to evaluating resources and climate. Homesteaders base their evaluation on their overall philosophy of sustainable living, including off-grid living, regenerative agriculture, or promoting ecological stewardship. This alignment guarantees that the site selected is appropriate for the homesteader's long-term goals and for meeting their present requirements.

To sum up, evaluating climate and resources is a dynamic and complex process that calls for a thorough understanding of a variety of topics, including ecosystem health, microbial diversity, geological features, sunlight patterns, wind dynamics, soil fertility, climatic factors, water resources, and long-term sustainability objectives. Homesteaders set out on this evaluation journey to promote resilience, live in harmony with the environment, and build a sustainable home that fulfills their goals and values. Their deliberate and comprehensive approach establishes a regenerative and long-lasting link between homesteaders and the land they call home.

3.3 Setting Realistic Goals

One of the most important stages of homestead planning is creating a realistic target list that will guide the path toward sustainable living. The procedure includes carefully analyzing each person's goals and the location's capabilities and incorporating sustainable practices. Homesteaders traverse this stage to develop a resilient and attainable vision for their homestead, motivated by a desire for environmental harmony and self-sufficiency.

Making Personal Goals Clear:

Analyzing one's desires in-depth is the first step toward setting realistic goals. Homesteaders describe their goals for the homestead, including how they see their everyday lives and what it means to be self-sufficient. This process includes determining certain lifestyle choices, beliefs, and preferences that will influence the homestead's objectives. Whether the emphasis is on raising animals, cultivating food, or embracing off-grid life, defining personal goals lays the groundwork for meaningful and attainable objectives.

Evaluating Resources and Skill Sets:

Setting realistic goals requires carefully evaluating each person's skill level and the resources at hand. Homesteaders assess their knowledge, proficiency, and useful skills in sustainable living. They assess their available resources, such as their money and time resources, as well as their access to tools and equipment. This self-reflective assessment ensures that objectives match the homesteader's skills and lays the groundwork for a practical and doable execution strategy.

Giving Sustainability Practices Top Priority:

The process of establishing goals starts to revolve around sustainability strategies. Practices that support the homestead's overall sustainability and are consistent with their ideals are given priority by homesteaders. This might include adopting waste minimization techniques, regenerative agricultural methods, water conservation plans, and renewable energy adoption. Setting sustainability practices as a top priority guarantees that objectives are both reachable and consistent with ecological principles, promoting a regenerative and peaceful coexistence with the land.

Harmonizing Short- and Long-Term Objectives:

Achieving a balance between short- and long-term goals is essential to setting realistic goals. Homesteaders set short-term objectives, such as starting a vegetable garden, constructing rudimentary infrastructure, or installing water collecting devices, that they can accomplish in the first year or two. At the same time, they outline long-term goals that might take several years to accomplish, such as creating agroforestry systems, becoming energy-independent, or growing livestock operations. This two-pronged strategy offers a path that permits gradual advancement while maintaining focus on the main objectives of sustainability.

Taking the Climate and Environment Into Account:

Setting realistic goals is always influenced by the local environment and climate of the selected site. When determining their objectives, homesteaders take the climate, the qualities of the soil, and other environmental factors into account. For instance, drought-resistant crops and water-efficient irrigation methods should be prioritized in areas with restricted water supplies. Homesteaders ensure their objectives are tailored to the particular possibilities and difficulties given by their homestead's particular setting by considering climatic and environmental variables.

Determining Metrics and Benchmarks:

Homesteaders set precise goals with measurable objectives to monitor their development and maintain responsibility. Whether measuring food production, energy savings, or the effective use of a permaculture design, having defined metrics enables impartial assessment. Homesteaders create attainable benchmarks to celebrate each little accomplishment toward the larger goal of sustainable living.

Resource Allocation Made Sensibly:

Setting realistic goals entails judicious use of available resources, such as labor, capital, and time. Realizing that resources are limited, homesteaders choose priorities based on what they can afford to invest in their homestead. This might include implementing projects in phases, enlisting community involvement, or maximizing resource consumption using sustainable technology. The aim is to ensure every part of the homestead gets the care and funding needed for a successful development.

Modifying Objectives to Fit Changing Situations:

Realism in goal-setting requires both adaptation and flexibility. Homesteaders understand that things might change for various reasons, such as unforeseen difficulties, changing priorities, or changes in the surrounding environment. Establishing realistic objectives requires allowing for the freedom to review and modify them as necessary. Using an adaptive strategy, the homestead is guaranteed to maintain its adaptability and resilience to the changing demands of sustainable living.

Promoting the Integration of the Whole:

Setting realistic goals entails promoting overall integration rather than just focusing on certain household aspects. The goal of homesteaders is to bring together many facets of their vision for a sustainable life. For instance, waste reduction tactics, water conservation measures, and energy efficiency programs are all incorporated with the aims of sustainable agriculture. Using a comprehensive approach, the homestead is guaranteed to function as a single unit, with every objective enhancing the resilience and sustainability of the ecosystem as a whole.

Accepting Ongoing Education:

The path to sustainable living is an ongoing educational process. Setting realistic goals recognizes the need for constant learning and adjustment. Homesteaders have an attitude of constant learning, keeping up with emerging sustainable practices, technological advancements, and neighborhood projects. This dedication to education guarantees that objectives are kept abreast of the most recent developments and breakthroughs in sustainable living.

In summary, realistic goal-setting in homestead planning is a deliberate and thoughtful process that includes defining personal objectives, evaluating skill sets and available resources, giving priority to sustainable practices, striking a balance between short- and long-term objectives, taking climate and environmental factors into account, defining precise metrics and milestones, allocating resources sensibly, modifying goals in response to changing conditions, promoting holistic integration, and embracing continuous learning. By using this all-encompassing strategy, homesteaders design a road map that is consistent with their beliefs, flexible enough to accommodate the ever-changing demands of sustainable living, and leads to a robust and rewarding homesteading experience.

Below is a text-based representation summarizing the key points for setting realistic goals in planning a homestead:

Key Points for Setting Realistic Goals in Homestead Planning

❖ **Clarifying Personal Aspirations:**

- Articulate a vision for self-sufficiency and sustainable living.

- Identify values, preferences, and lifestyle choices.

❖ **Assessing Skill Sets and Resources:**

- Evaluate individual knowledge, expertise, and practical skills.

- Take stock of financial resources, time commitments, and available tools.

❖ **Prioritizing Sustainability Practices:**

- Align goals with sustainable practices that reflect values.

- Emphasize regenerative agriculture, water conservation, and waste reduction.

❖ **Balancing Short-Term and Long-Term Goals:**

- Define immediate goals achievable within the first years.

- Articulate long-term visions that may take several years to realize.

❖ **Considering Climate and Environmental Factors:**

- Factor in local climate conditions, soil characteristics, and environmental variables.

- Adapt goals to address specific challenges and opportunities of the chosen location.

❖ **Establishing Clear Metrics and Milestones:**

- Define specific metrics to track progress objectively.

- Set achievable milestones to celebrate incremental progress.

❖ **Allotting Resources Wisely:**

- Wisely allocate time, money, and labor to different goals.

- Consider phased implementation, community support, and sustainable technologies.

- ❖ **Adapting Goals to Changing Circumstances:**

  - Build flexibility into goals to adapt to unexpected challenges.

  - Reassess and adjust goals as circumstances evolve.

- ❖ **Fostering Holistic Integration:**

  - Create synergy among different aspects of sustainable living.

  - Integrate goals related to agriculture, energy efficiency, water conservation, and waste reduction.

- ❖ **Embracing Continuous Learning:**

  - Acknowledge the continuous learning nature of sustainable living.

  - Stay informed about new practices, technologies, and community initiatives.

This table summarizes the key considerations for setting realistic goals in the planning of a homestead, providing a comprehensive guide for homesteaders to create a sustainable and fulfilling living space.

3.4 Budgeting for Homesteading

A key component of the planning process is creating a budget for homesteading, which calls for careful evaluation of available funds to turn an idea for sustainable living into an actual, attainable goal. Aspiring homesteaders set out on this financial adventure, knowing that prudent budgeting is about matching spending to the principles and objectives guiding their homesteading endeavor and controlling expenses.

Setting Financial Objectives:

Setting defined financial objectives is the first step in creating a homesteading budget. Homesteaders voice their vision for the homestead, defining immediate and long-term goals. These objectives include a wide range of topics, such as continuing maintenance, sustainable practices, infrastructure development, and land acquisition. Homesteaders establish a budget that fits their overall goal of living a self-sufficient and sustainable lifestyle by outlining particular financial goals.

Evaluating the Need for Initial Investment:

Starting a homestead sometimes necessitates an upfront investment to obtain property, construct infrastructure, and put the fundamentals of sustainable living into practice. Homesteaders evaluate these demands in great detail, considering expenses like buying or leasing land, building supplies, tools, and machinery. This budgeting stage is essential for figuring out the amount of money needed to establish the foundation for a successful homesteading endeavor.

Formulating an All-Inclusive Budget:

A detailed budget is the homesteader's financial roadmap. Homesteaders divide their costs into many categories according to their vision: livestock, agriculture, energy systems, water management, and continuing upkeep. Budgetary allocations are made to each category, guaranteeing that priorities disperse funds. Homesteaders who have a well-organized budget are better able to make wise choices, stay out of debt, and anticipate problems before they arise.

Sustainable Practice Accounting:

Homesteading is centered on sustainable living, and budgeting is dedicated to eco-friendly methods. Homesteaders raised money for environmentally friendly projects, including organic agricultural methods, renewable energy systems, permaculture design, and water conservation techniques. The long-term advantages of these practices—such as lower utility bills and more self-sufficiency—make them indispensable to the homesteading budget despite their possible upfront expenses.

Finding a Balance Between Short- and Long-Term Investments:

Achieving a balance between immediate investments and long-term sustainability is crucial when creating a homesteading budget. Long-term investments include solar panels, water harvesting systems, and durable equipment; short-term investments include garden tools, seeds, and basic infrastructure. This delicate balancing exercise guarantees that funds are allotted to address urgent needs while enhancing the homestead's long-term resilience.

Taking Unexpected Costs and Contingencies Into Account:

Prudent budgeting considers uncertainty by setting aside money for unanticipated costs and situations. Homesteaders know unforeseen difficulties like equipment failures or severe weather might occur. A financial safety net is provided by allocating a percentage of the budget for contingencies, allowing homesteaders to handle unanticipated events without jeopardizing the homestead's overall stability.

Giving Cost-Reduction and Self-Sufficiency Priority:

Budgeting shows that homesteaders are committed to becoming self-sufficient. Setting aside money for investments that help people become less dependent on outside sources aligns with developing a self-sufficient way of life. Investments in food production, energy independence, and waste reduction techniques are budgetary choices that may improve self-sufficiency while lowering costs over the long run.

Examining Options for Sustainable Financing:

Homesteaders look into sustainable funding choices that fit with their ideals in addition to conventional financing techniques. Investigating grants, subsidies, or community-based funding programs that assist sustainable living projects may fall within this category. Homesteaders may increase their financial ability to adopt environmentally friendly practices and accomplish their aims of sustainable living by using these other sources of income.

Putting Development-Phased Budgeting Into Practice:

Budgeting takes this gradual approach into account since homesteading is often a staged development process. Homesteaders use a phased budgeting approach rather than trying to adopt all components of the homestead at once. To allow for progressive growth and ensure that financial resources are optimal for each step of the homesteading journey entails prioritizing and budgeting for various periods of development.

Monitoring and Assessing Expenses:

A homesteading budget that works involves systems for monitoring and assessing expenses. Homesteaders keep thorough records of all their financial dealings, routinely compare their expenditures to their budgetary allotments, and make any necessary plan adjustments. This continuous review is a financial management tool that improves the homestead's overall sustainability and success by ensuring the budget is dynamic and adaptable to changing conditions.

Looking for Cooperation and Support from the Community:

Homesteaders understand the value of teamwork and community cooperation when creating a budget for sustainable living. Joint purchasing, pooling of resources, or sharing of equipment are examples of collaborative projects that may drastically lower personal financial obligations. Through the power of a strong community, homesteaders increase their potential as a group to accomplish common sustainability objectives.

Combining Learning and Developing Skills:

Investments in education and skill development are included in the budgeting process for homesteading, in addition to financial concerns. Homesteaders set aside money for courses, instructional materials, and other initiatives that advance their understanding of and skill with sustainable techniques. Long-term self-sufficiency is facilitated by this educational investment, which also gives homesteaders the flexibility and creativity they need to advance toward sustainable living.

To sum up, homesteading budgeting is a thorough and strategic process that includes setting financial objectives, determining the amount of initial investment required, drafting a detailed budget, accounting for sustainable practices, weighing the pros and cons of short- and long-term investments, planning for emergencies, putting self-sufficiency first, looking into sustainable financing options, putting phased development into place, monitoring and analyzing spending, enlisting the help of the community, and incorporating education and skill development. Homesteaders create the foundation for a robust and sustainable living experience that embodies their goals and beliefs via careful financial planning.

3.5 Establishing a Sustainable Homestead Design

Designing a sustainable farm is one of the most important steps to environmental harmony and self-sufficiency. This procedure entails carefully integrating ecological concepts, resource efficiency, and constructing a sturdy and useful living area. Homesteaders go into the design process knowing that their homestead's sustainability and success will be greatly impacted by their infrastructure, landscape, and layout decisions.

Combining the Principles of Permaculture:

The use of permaculture principles forms the foundation of any sustainable homestead design. The terms "permanent culture" and "permanent agriculture" refer to a design philosophy called "permaculture," which creates regenerative and productive environments by imitating natural ecosystems. Homesteaders arrange their property using permaculture concepts like variety, observation, and interdependence. They strategically choose where to put cattle, crops, and orchards to optimize sustainability and efficiency.

Functional and Efficient Zoning:

A key idea in permaculture design is zoning, which involves arranging various spaces according to energy flow and usefulness. Homesteaders assign zones based on the frequency of usage and level of administration. Herbs and vegetable gardens may be found in Zone 1, nearest the residential area. In contrast, natural and undeveloped areas are kept in Zone 5, the least controlled region. By using time and resources best, this zoning technique produces a design that adheres to sustainability standards.

Applying Agroforestry Techniques:

Incorporating trees and shrubs into agricultural systems, or agroforestry, is crucial to sustainable homestead design. Homesteaders thoughtfully plant trees to provide a variety of functions, such as windbreaks, shade, and animal habitat. Alley cropping, windbreak construction, and silvopasture are examples of agroforestry techniques that improve biodiversity, preserve soil, and strengthen the homestead's long-term resilience.

Creating Landscapes with Minimal Water Use:

Water is a valuable resource in homesteading, and sustainable design includes techniques to maximize its usage. Water may be effectively captured and distributed across the landscape using rain gardens, contour planting, and swales. Homesteaders create landscapes that improve soil and plant health, decrease runoff, and promote water retention. The objective is to develop a water-efficient design that encourages sustainable water management and reduces reliance on outside water sources.

Putting Regenerative Agriculture into Practice:

Using regenerative agricultural techniques is essential to designing a sustainable homestead. To improve the fertility and health of their soil, homesteaders use practices including cover crops, rotational grazing, and no-till farming. These measures support agriculture's long-term sustainability by improving the land's resilience and sequestering carbon. Recognizing the importance of regenerative agriculture in supporting robust homesteads and healthy ecosystems, the design incorporates it as a central component.

Constructing Green Structures:

Beyond aesthetics, the homestead's buildings are designed with sustainability and eco-friendliness as top priorities. Homesteaders prefer low-impact materials, such as sustainable bamboo, recycled metal, and recovered wood. Passive solar design techniques are included to optimize natural heating and cooling and minimize dependency on artificial energy sources. Sustainable design principles are reflected in the layout of environmentally friendly buildings, which result in environments that are harmonious with their surroundings.

Considering Energy Efficiency in Design:

An essential component of a sustainable household design is energy efficiency. Homesteaders evaluate a building's orientation to maximize solar radiation and minimize the need for artificial heating and lighting. To provide electricity for the household, renewable energy sources like solar and wind turbines are cleverly combined. The design seeks to decrease energy use through intelligent planning, energy-efficient appliances, and insulation, resulting in a low-impact and sustainable energy profile.

Developing Effective Waste Management Frameworks:

Sustainable homesteading requires effective waste management, and solutions for minimizing, reusing, and recycling trash are included in the design. Greywater systems recover water from everyday activities for irrigation, while composting stations are carefully positioned for organic waste. By prioritizing the circular economy in their waste management system design, homesteaders ensure that trash becomes a resource rather than a burden on the environment.

Including Animals in Holistic Designs:

Including animals in the architecture of homesteads that house cattle is crucial. The principles of holistic management guide decisions on livestock housing, pasture management, and rotational grazing. The design promotes a healthy and regenerating ecology by considering the symbiotic link between plants and animals. A homestead design incorporates livestock in a manner that improves soil fertility, reduces environmental impact, and fosters the welfare of both plants and animals.

Making Plans to Preserve Biodiversity and Habitats:

An ecosystem on a homestead that is robust and healthy must have biodiversity. Sustainable design creates habitats for animals, birds, and beneficial insects by incorporating techniques to protect and improve biodiversity. The design incorporates hedgerows, wild spaces, and native plants to provide habitat for various species. Intentional design for biodiversity supports pollination, natural pest management, and the general health of ecosystems.

Adopting Scalable and Modular Design:

A modular and scalable design philosophy that promotes flexibility and expansion is central to sustainable homestead architecture. Raised beds, rainwater collection systems, and composting spaces are modular design components that may be added to or modified in response to changing demands. This scalability supports flexibility and ongoing development in response to new objectives or difficulties by accommodating changes that occur in the system over time.

Including Recreational and Aesthetic Areas:

A sustainable homestead design prioritizes sustainability and utility but acknowledges the value of aesthetic and leisure areas. The homestead is more enjoyable and well-rounded by thoughtful landscaping, outdoor leisure areas, and communal meeting places. A feeling of connection to the natural environment is fostered, and the quality of life on the homestead is improved by including aesthetics and enjoyment in the design.

To sum up, creating a sustainable homestead design involves a deliberate and comprehensive approach that incorporates various elements such as agroforestry techniques, water-efficient landscapes, regenerative agriculture, eco-friendly buildings, energy efficiency, effective waste management, planning for biodiversity, modular and scalable design, and visually pleasing and recreational areas. A complete approach ensures that the design aligns with the homesteader's ideals and objectives, resulting in a durable and peaceful living place that benefits the environment and its occupants.

Chapter 4: Sustainable Agriculture

4.1 Introduction to Permaculture

Derived from "permanent agriculture" or "permanent culture," permaculture is a comprehensive and regenerative design method that aims to build self-sufficient and sustainable ecosystems. Bill Mollison and David Holmgren first presented permaculture in the 1970s, emphasizing the peaceful coexistence of people, landscapes, and sustainable agricultural concepts. It goes beyond traditional farming methods. This overview of permaculture explores its guiding concepts, ethics in design, and how it has revolutionized sustainable agricultural methods.

Fundamental Ideas of Permaculture:

Three fundamental ideas underpin permaculture and form the basis of its design philosophy:

Earth care: Permaculture emphasizes actions that support and revitalize the natural world, placing a high importance on environmental sustainability. This idea highlights how all living things are interrelated and how our duty as stewards of the planet is to care for it.

Care for People: The goal of permaculture is to create a society in which people coexist peacefully. This concept strongly emphasizes addressing human needs to ensure social justice, equitable resource distribution, and the development of supportive and equitable communities.

Return of Surplus or Fair Share: The notion of a fair share centers on reducing consumption and giving back excess resources to the environment and society. The goal of permaculture is to design systems that benefit human civilization and the larger ecology and are sustainable.

Ethic Design:

Three interconnected ethics serve as the cornerstone of permaculture, directing decision-making and the application of design:

Earth Care: The significance of protecting and replenishing the natural environment is emphasized by this ethic. Maintaining the Earth's health and vitality entails soil protection, water management, and biodiversity preservation.

People Care The second ethic concerns providing for people's necessities while promoting positive interpersonal social interactions. It entails developing structures that prioritize communities and people's empowerment and well-being.

Fair Share: The fair share ethic promotes equitable resource allocation and considers the Earth and the larger community when making decisions. It opposes the notion of overconsumption and promotes resource management that is thoughtful and balanced.

Permaculture Design Principles:

Using a set of design principles, permaculture offers a framework for building robust and sustainable systems. Several essential design tenets comprise:

Observation: Permaculturists carefully observe the natural environment, climate, and existing ecosystems before making any alterations. This in-depth knowledge guarantees that actions are appropriate for the context and guide design choices.

Collection and Store Energy: Efficient energy collection and storage in a variety of ways is promoted by permaculture. This entails collecting rainwater, using renewable energy sources, and strategically placing plants and buildings to maximize sunlight.

Exercise Self-Control and Take Feedback: Permaculture designs are flexible and receptive to community and environmental input. This idea highlights how crucial it is to continually evaluate and modify systems in light of their effectiveness and impact.

Employ and Worth Renewable Resources and Services: Using naturally replenishable resources is encouraged by permaculture. This entails putting renewable resources ahead of limited ones, employing organic matter for soil fertility, and capturing sun and wind energy.

Permaculturists tackle design by identifying and comprehending overarching patterns before focusing on particular specifics. This all-encompassing viewpoint guarantees that the entire structure is in harmony with natural patterns and operates as a whole.

Sectors and Zones of Permaculture:

In permaculture, items are arranged inside a design according to their frequency of usage and degree of control via a zoning system. These five zones, which go from 0 to 5, are set up like this:

Zone 0: High-intensity management and activities occur in the house or central living area.

Zone 1: The areas next to the house that need regular care, such as small animals and kitchen gardens.

Zone 2: Managed habitats, which might contain animals that need less regular care and bigger gardens and orchards.

Zone 3: Bigger farms or managed woodlands that need sporadic maintenance.

Zone 4: Areas that are semi-wild and have seen little human intrusion, used for forestry or foraging.

Zone 5: Natural places that have not been impacted by human activity, such as wilderness.

Sectors are other outside factors that are taken into account in permaculture design. Sunlight, wind direction, water movement, and other natural elements that affect the overall design are some examples.

Bringing Plants and Animals Together:

The integration of plants and animals in a manner that resembles natural ecosystems is encouraged by permaculture. This comprises agroforestry techniques that include growing trees and shrubs next to crops and companion planting, which involves growing plants mutually beneficial to one another. Having animals around, like goats to manage weeds or hens to control pests, helps create a comprehensive and integrated approach to sustainable agriculture.

Food Guilds and Forests:

Building food forests that resemble natural forests in form and function is a key component of permaculture. Tall trees, smaller fruit trees, bushes, herbaceous plants, ground coverings, and root crops are among the several layers of vegetation that make up food forests. These systems' design goals are to increase resilience, production, and biodiversity.

Another permaculture idea is guilds, which plant combinations of species that complement one another. Plants that fix nitrogen, dynamic accumulators, insect-repelling herbs, and fruit-bearing trees are a few examples of these guilds. The synergies between guild members improve the general health and productivity of the system.

Putting Water Harvesting and Conservation into Practice:

Water is emphasized as a valuable resource in permaculture design, incorporating techniques for gathering and conserving water. Water is effectively captured and stored using swales, contour planting, and rainwater collecting systems. Permaculture techniques support sustainable water management by creating landscapes that encourage water retention and lessen runoff.

Developing Healthy Soils:

A key component of permaculture is healthy soil, and methods focus on enhancing and preserving the fertility and structure of the soil: mulching, cover crops, and composting increase microbial activity and soil organic matter. Regenerative farming methods are valued highly by permaculturists since they maintain and gradually enhance soil health.

Urban Permaculture: A Look Inside

Although permaculture is often linked with rural areas, urban settings may equally benefit from its principles. Urban permaculture encompasses innovative approaches to sustainable urban living, such as vertical farming, rooftop gardens, and community-supported agriculture. Urban environments may benefit from permaculture concepts, including waste reduction, biodiversity enhancement, and effective resource utilization.

Community Involvement and Permaculture:

In addition to being a collection of design guidelines, permaculture is a way of thinking that promotes cooperation and community involvement. Permaculture practices, such as communal gardens, local food programs, and community-supported agriculture (CSA), promote community self-sufficiency and resilience.

The Impact of Permaculture Worldwide:

Globally, permaculture is becoming increasingly popular as a sustainable way of farming and living. Its ideas are practiced in various cultural and climatic contexts, meeting local needs and advancing global sustainability. The number of projects and courses focused on permaculture design has increased, fostering the development of a community of practitioners dedicated to regenerative methods.

To sum up, this introduction to permaculture offers a basis for comprehending its fundamental ideas, design ethics, and revolutionary influence on sustainable agriculture. Permaculture, which has its roots in ecological harmony, provides a thorough framework for creating resilient and regenerative systems that put the needs of people, the environment, and fair sharing first. As an all-encompassing approach to sustainable living, permaculture continues to motivate a worldwide shift toward regenerative methods that promote community well-being and environmental responsibility.

4.2 Organic Farming Practices

A key component of sustainable agriculture is organic farming, which emphasizes biodiversity, environmental management, and the health of the land and the customer. Unlike conventional farming, which often uses artificial fertilizers and pesticides, organic farming emphasizes ecological balance, natural processes, and a comprehensive approach to farming. This investigation of organic farming methods explores this sustainable agriculture paradigm's ideas, methods, and advantages.

Fertility and Soil Health:

A deep regard for the fertility and health of the soil is fundamental to organic farming. Organic farmers understand that soil is a dynamic environment full of beneficial insects, fungi, and microorganisms. Crop rotation, cover crops, organic matter, and compost are used in place of synthetic fertilizers in organic methods to promote and preserve soil health.

Compost: Compost is a rich source of organic matter and nutrients organic farmers use. Plant and animal wastes are broken down throughout the composting process to produce a humus-rich, nutrient-dense material that improves soil fertility and structure.

Planting certain crops to cover and safeguard the soil while the primary cash crop is dormant is known as cover cropping. These cover crops increase biodiversity, stop soil erosion, and contribute organic matter.

Crop rotation is a technique organic farmers use to reduce the burden of pests and diseases and avoid the loss of soil nutrients. Crop rotation in a deliberate order breaks pest cycles and improves soil fertility overall.

Management of Diseases and Pests:

Integrated pest management (IPM) techniques are used in organic farming to control diseases and pests without artificial pesticides. To sustain a resilient and healthy environment, these measures prioritize cultural practices, biological control, and prevention.

Biological Control: To organically manage pest populations, beneficial insects like ladybugs and predatory beetles are imported or fostered. This method uses the ecosystem's strength to preserve a natural equilibrium.

Companion planting: In organic farming, it's standard practice to plant some crops next to one other to promote growth or deter pests. To discourage nematodes, for instance, marigolds are often interplanted with vegetables.

Disease-resistant types: To minimize the need for chemical treatments, organic farmers choose crop types that show innate resistance to prevalent illnesses.

Crop Diversity: Various cropping techniques reduce the possibility of extensive pest or disease outbreaks. An ecosystem becomes more robust and complicated when there are many crops present.

Controlling Weeds:

In organic farming, weed management is accomplished using mechanical techniques, cultural approaches, and the cultivation of crops that restrict weed growth. Different methods are used instead of herbicides to keep fields free of weeds.

Mulching: By forming a physical barrier, organic mulches, such as wood chips or straw, can inhibit the development of weeds. Mulching also controls soil temperature and moisture retention.

Mechanical Cultivation: Organic farmers use cultivation instruments to keep weeds under control without using pesticides. Soil cultivation increases soil aeration and inhibits the development of weeds.

Some organic farmers use flame weeding, in which the crop rows are covered with a controlled flame that kills and scorches immature weeds without chemical pesticides.

Heirloom and non-GMO varieties:

Genetically modified organisms (GMOs) are not used in organic farming, and traditional types are often preferred. Organic principles, which emphasize natural and traditional breeding techniques, align with non-GMO seeds, guaranteeing that crops are developed without genetic changes.

Open-pollinated kinds, known as heirloom seeds, have been handed down through the generations. The distinct tastes, versatility, and genetic variety shown by these cultivars often aid in conserving agricultural legacy.

Steer clear of artificial inputs:

The rejection of synthetic inputs, including fertilizers, herbicides, and pesticides, is a hallmark of organic farming. Rather, natural solutions that respect ecological principles and lessen their influence on the environment are used by organic farmers.

Natural Fertilizers: Compost, manure, and organic amendments are natural fertilizers that organic farmers use for their crops. Without raising the danger of chemical runoff, these inputs improve soil fertility.

Natural Pest Control: Organic farming uses natural pest control techniques instead of synthetic ones. This strategy encourages a stronger and more resilient environment while preserving beneficial insects.

Non-toxic Herbicides: As an alternative to synthetic herbicides, non-toxic herbicides like organic oils or solutions based on acetic acid may be used to manage weeds in organic farming.

Standards and Certification:

For farming practices to be labeled as organic, they must go through certification procedures and meet mandatory requirements. Obtaining certification guarantees that farmers who practice organic farming adhere to organic principles and fulfill certain requirements for soil health, insect control, and the avoidance of synthetic inputs. Customers may shop with confidence, knowing that the items they buy are made in compliance with organic agricultural standards thanks to this certification.

Biodiversity and Conservation:

Organic agricultural methods actively aid the protection of biodiversity. Organic farmers cultivate habitats that sustain various species, from helpful insects to soil microbes, by avoiding synthetic pesticides that might damage non-target creatures. In addition to its inherent ecological advantages, biodiversity is important for pollination and natural pest management.

Regional and Ecological Methods:

Organic farming often complies with sustainable and local agricultural practices. Local markets are given priority by many organic farmers, which lowers the transportation sector's carbon impact. Furthermore, organic agricultural methods use sustainable measures like energy efficiency and water conservation to reduce their environmental effect.

Equitable Trade and Social Responsibility:

Organic farming is often associated with more general ethical and social concerns. Fairtrade principles are embraced by many organic farms, guaranteeing fair salaries, safe working conditions, and ethical treatment of farm workers. Organic farming strongly emphasizes social responsibility, which goes beyond environmental concerns to include the welfare of the communities engaged in the farming process.

Advantages for Consumer Health:

The claimed health advantages of organic food are a major factor in customer choice. Using organic agricultural methods, food is produced without artificial pesticides or residues, lowering the possible health concerns of being around them. It's also thought that several minerals and antioxidants are present in greater concentrations in organic crops.

Obstacles and Rebuttals:

Organic farming is praised for its positive effects on the environment and human health, but it is not without difficulties and detractors. According to some detractors, organic farming produces less efficiently than conventional farming, which might result in greater costs and less scalability. Furthermore, there have been discussions on the suitability of the existing organic standards, and definitions of what is "organic" might differ across nations and areas.

Prospects for Organic Farming Going Forward:

Organic farming must continue its research and innovation to overcome obstacles and improve sustainability. Technological, agroecological, and regenerative practice advancements portend well for the sustained expansion and development of organic farming. Optimizing organic farming systems will need to combine conventional knowledge with cutting-edge approaches in light of the changing global agricultural environment and climate.

To summarize, organic farming methods are dedicated to regenerative and sustainable agriculture. Organic farming offers a strong alternative to conventional techniques since it is based on concepts that prioritize soil health, biodiversity, and ecological balance. Organic farming is increasingly important in promoting a healthier world and a more sustainable food system as consumer awareness and environmental concerns develop.

4.3 Crop Rotation and Companion Planting

Companion planting and crop rotation are fundamental to sustainable farming systems. These strategies provide natural and comprehensive ways to improve soil fertility, control pests, and support the ecosystem's health, going beyond the traditional strategy of continuous monoculture and synthetic chemical usage. This examination of companion planting and crop rotation explores its tenets, advantages, and significant influence on sustainable agriculture.

Rotation of crops:

The systematic process of planting several crops in a predetermined order across multiple seasons is known as crop rotation. Crop rotation is based on not growing the same crop in the same soil yearly. Rather, a precise sequence of crops is sown to disrupt the cycles of pests and diseases, maximize nutrient uptake, and enhance the general health of the soil.

Important Crop Rotation Components:

Diversity: By introducing various plant species into the soil via crop rotation, pests and diseases unique to a certain crop are kept at bay. Because different crops need different amounts of nutrients, there is less chance of soil depletion.

Cycle of Nutrients: Diverse crops take in and release distinct nutrients from the soil. Farmers may increase soil fertility naturally and without artificial fertilizers by rotating crops with different nutrient requirements. This helps to maintain a balanced nutrient cycle.

Management of Pests and Diseases: Crop rotation breaks the life cycles of pests and diseases unique to a certain crop. For instance, a pest that preys on a certain crop could not find adequate hosts the next year, which would lower its population.

Weed Control: Certain crops are better than others at keeping weeds at bay. Crop rotation may include crops with potent weed-suppressing qualities to aid in natural weed management.

A Simple Crop Rotation Plan Example

- ★ *Year 1:* Depletes nitrogen in corn
- ★ *Year 2:* Fix nitrogen with legumes
- ★ *Year 3:* Pest-Repelling Brassicas
- ★ *Year 4:* Root Crops (Pest Cycle Breaking)
- ★ Grains (Restore soil structure) in Year Five

The advantages of crop rotation

Crop rotation breaks the life cycles of pests and diseases, which lessens the need for chemical interventions in pest and disease control. An ecology for farming that is healthier and more robust benefits from this natural method.

Management of Nutrients: The needs for various nutrients differ throughout crops. Crop rotation prevents nutrient depletion and increases overall soil fertility by balancing the nutrients in the soil.

Better Soil Structure: By breaking up compacted soil, deep-rooted crops planted in rotation may improve root penetration and water infiltration. This lowers the chance of erosion and improves the general soil structure.

Weed Suppression: Some crops in a rotation can inhibit the development of weeds, which lessens their competition for resources and nutrients. This helps keep weeds under control without using pesticides.

Sustainability: By reducing the negative effects of agriculture on the environment, crop rotation is consistent with sustainable agricultural techniques. It encourages the development of a more resilient and balanced agroecosystem and lessens the need for artificial inputs.

Planting companions:

The deliberate placement of several plant species to promote one another's development, ward off pests, and boost crop health is known as companion planting. This age-old farming method uses the symbiotic connections that certain plants have with one another to create a peaceful and advantageous environment.

Important Companion Planting Components:

Certain plants emit substances that can repel certain types of pests. Companion planting helps shield nearby crops from insect infestations using these inherent qualities.

Advantageous Insects: Specific plants attract advantageous insects that feed on common pests. Farmers support an ecosystem's natural balance by planting insect-attracting plants next to crops vulnerable to pest infestations.

Fixation of Nitrogen: Leguminous plants can fix nitrogen from the soil. These nitrogen-fixing plants are used in companion planting to increase soil fertility and provide nearby crops with nutrients.

Space Utilization: By combining plants with distinct growth tendencies, companion planting makes the most use of available space—taller plants, for instance, shade shorter, more sun-sensitive plants.

Examples of Planting Companions:

Basil with tomatoes: Certain pests that often harm tomatoes are repelled by basil. Basil plants may help shield tomatoes from insect infestations.

Corn, beans, and squash are planted together in a method known as "three sisters planting," which dates back to Native American planting customs. Beans replenish nitrogen in the soil, corn helps beans climb, and squash is a ground cover to keep weeds down.

Vegetables with Marigolds: Marigolds emit substances that ward against nematodes and pests in the soil. One way to prevent nematode damage to vegetable root systems is to interplant marigolds with them.

Companion planting improves soil fertility in orchards by placing nitrogen-fixing cover crops, such as clover, under fruit trees. Furthermore, blooming plants attract pollinators, which enhances fruit yield.

Advantages of Planting Companions:

Natural Pest Control: Using certain plants' ability to repel pests, companion planting can lessen the need for synthetic pesticides. This encourages using a more ecologically friendly and sustainable pest control method.

Enhanced Soil Fertility: Nitrogen-fixing companion plants improve soil fertility by making more nitrogen available for nearby crops. As a result, less synthetic fertilizer is needed.

Enhanced Biodiversity: Planting companion plants brings a variety of plant species together nearby. A wider variety of helpful insects and microbes are supported by this diversity, which enhances the general health of the environment.

Higher Yields: Healthier crops and higher yields may result from companion plants' synergistic interactions. For instance, since beans boost nitrogen availability, planting beans next to maize may increase corn yields.

Space Efficiency: Companion planting makes the most of available space by carefully matching plants with growth patterns that are complementary to one another. This is especially useful for little agricultural areas or gardens.

Obstacles & Things to Think About:

Although companion planting and crop rotation have many advantages, there are drawbacks and difficulties in putting these strategies into reality. Several things are necessary for success, including careful planning, understanding plant interactions, and environmental adaptability.

Planning: Careful planning is necessary for effective crop rotation and companion planting since each crop has unique requirements and features. Farmers must develop strategies considering insect susceptibility, nutritional needs, and development patterns.

Knowledge: For implementation to be effective, a thorough grasp of soil dynamics, insect behavior, and plant relationships is required. Farmers must always learn about the unique requirements of various crops and how they might work harmoniously.

Adaptation: Variations may be seen in the local climate, soil properties, and insect pressures. Farmers must modify crop rotation and companion planting techniques to fit the unique circumstances of their area.

Trial and error: Crop rotation and companion planting are two agricultural strategies that often include some trial and error. It could be necessary for farmers to test out several combinations to find the one that best suits their unique situation.

Integration with Other Practices: The best results from crop rotation and companion planting come from its combination with other environmentally friendly farming techniques, including cover crops, organic fertilizer, and water conservation. An agricultural system that is more robust and sustainable is the result of a comprehensive strategy that considers many variables.

In summary:

To sum up, crop rotation and companion planting are essential elements of sustainable agriculture, representing values that support soil health, ecological balance, and organic pest control. These methods, rooted in millennia of agricultural knowledge, provide respectable alternatives for chemical-intensive farming and traditional monoculture. Agriculture has the potential to become more resilient, sustainable, and biodiversity-rich as long as farmers and researchers keep experimenting with and improving these methods. By carefully combining companion planting with crop rotation, farmers can create a more sustainable and healthful food system that will benefit future generations.

4.3 Crop Rotation and Companion Planting

1. Crop Rotation	2. Companion Planting
Principles of Crop Rotation:	*Principles of Companion Planting:*
- Diversity: Introduce a variety of plant species to prevent pest and disease buildup.	- Pest Repellent Properties: Certain plants release compounds to deter pests.
- Nutrient Cycling: Balance nutrient levels by rotating crops with different nutrient needs.	- Beneficial Insects: Attract insects that prey on pests to maintain a natural balance.
- Pest and Disease Management: Disrupt life cycles to reduce the need for chemical interventions.	- Nitrogen Fixation: Include nitrogen-fixing plants to enhance soil fertility.
- Weed Control: Suppress weeds through natural means, contributing to weed control.	- Space Utilization: Maximize space by pairing plants with different growth habits.

Benefits of Crop Rotation:	**Benefits of Companion Planting:**
- Pest and Disease Control: Disrupts life cycles, reducing the need for chemical interventions.	- Natural Pest Control: Reduces reliance on synthetic pesticides through plant interactions.
- Nutrient Management: Balances nutrient levels, promoting overall soil fertility.	- Improved Soil Fertility: Nitrogen-fixing plants contribute to soil health and fertility.
- Improved Soil Structure: Deep-rooted crops enhance soil structure and reduce erosion.	- Enhanced Biodiversity: Encourages a diverse range of plant species, supporting ecosystem health.
- Weed Suppression: Minimizes weed growth through natural processes.	- Increased Yields: Synergistic relationships between plants can lead to higher yields.
- Sustainability: Aligns with sustainable practices, reducing environmental impact.	- Space Efficiency: Optimizes space utilization by strategically pairing plants.

Examples of Crop Rotation:	*Examples of Companion Planting:*
- Year 1: Corn (Depletes nitrogen)	- Tomatoes and Basil: Basil repels pests harmful to tomatoes.
- Year 2: Legumes (Fix nitrogen)	- Three Sisters Planting (Corn, Beans, Squash): Traditional Native American technique.
- Year 3: Brassicas (Repel pests)	- Marigolds and Vegetables: Marigolds deter nematodes harmful to vegetables.

- Year 4: Root Crops (Break pest cycles)	- Companion Planting in Orchards: Nitrogen-fixing covers crops beneath fruit trees.
- Year 5: Grains (Restore soil structure)	---

Challenges and Considerations:

- Planning: Requires careful planning considering growth patterns, nutrient needs, and pest susceptibility.

- Knowledge: Deep understanding of plant interactions, pest behaviors, and soil dynamics is crucial.

- Adaptation: Strategies need to be adapted to suit local climate, soil conditions, and pest pressures.

- Trial and Error: Often involves experimentation to determine the most effective combinations.

- Integration with Other Practices: Most effective when integrated with other sustainable farming practices.

4.4 Animal Husbandry and Integrated Livestock Management

Integrating livestock management and animal husbandry are essential elements of sustainable agriculture that provide a mutually beneficial link between agriculture and animal welfare. The concepts, procedures, and advantages of ethically rearing and incorporating animals into agricultural ecosystems are examined in this section. This all-encompassing strategy maximizes plant and animal productivity while promoting environmental sustainability, from pasture rotation to animal byproducts.

1. The Fundamentals of Animal Care:

Moral Care and Well-Being:

Animal welfare and ethical treatment are fundamental to animal agriculture. Humane treatment, having access to clean water, eating a healthy diet, and having enough room to live are priorities of sustainable practices. Animals are considered essential components of a sustainable and regenerative agricultural system, not merely commodities.

Systems Based on Pasture:

Systems based on pastures, in which animals have access to wide areas for grazing, are often used in sustainable animal husbandry. This encourages healthier animals, offers varied food, and imitates natural habits. Overgrazing is avoided, and natural forage regeneration is permitted by rotational grazing, where livestock are regularly transferred to new pasture areas.

Decreased Dependency on Hormones and Antibiotics:

Sustainable techniques seek to minimize the negative environmental effects of livestock production while maintaining animal health by reducing antibiotics and hormones. This means choosing breeds suited to the local area, maintaining hygienic living circumstances, and practicing good nutrition as preventative measures, all of which lessen the need for medicinal treatments.

2. Livestock Management Integrated:

Turning over grain:

One essential component of integrated livestock management is rotational grazing. Methodically, animals are rotated across various pastures or paddocks to promote vegetation regeneration and rest. This increases soil fertility by allowing manure to decompose and guarantees a steady fodder supply.

Nutritional Cycle:

The cycling of nutrients in agricultural systems is aided by livestock. When handled carefully, animal dung may be useful for agricultural fertilization. Integrating systems closes the nutrient loop and increases soil fertility without synthetic fertilizers using this nutrient-rich waste.

Stream Diversification of Income:

Farmers that practice integrated livestock management have the chance to diversify their revenue sources. In addition to the main goods like meat, milk, and eggs, leftovers like wool, dung, and feathers may be used or sold. This diversity improves the farm's overall sustainability and strengthens its economic resilience.

Diminished Ecological Effects:

Livestock may contribute to a lower environmental impact when they are integrated well. While the nutrient-rich manure improves soil fertility, managed grazing prevents overgrazing and soil degradation. This all-encompassing strategy lessens the detrimental ecological effects that large-scale, industrialized livestock production often brings about.

3. Practices for Sustainable Livestock:

Raised on pasture and fed grass:

Grass-fed and pasture-raised livestock systems are prioritized in sustainable livestock production. Because they feed on natural grasses, animals produce healthier meat and dairy products with better nutritional profiles. This method contrasts confined animal feeding operations (CAFOs), which house animals in cramped spaces and often feed them grain-based diets.

Traditions and Regional Breeds:

One of the main tenets of sustainable animal husbandry is the preservation and use of historical and regional breeds. These breeds often enhance biodiversity, are more disease-resistant, and are better suited to their particular locales. Encouraging a variety of breeds contributes to the preservation of genetic diversity in animal populations.

Comprehensive Veterinary Care:

Veterinary treatment should be approached holistically in sustainable livestock management. This covers precautionary steps, including healthy eating, having access to potable water, and managing parasites naturally. Integrative techniques are used in veterinary care to reduce the need for antibiotics and synthetic drugs, integrating traditional methods with alternative therapies like herbal therapy.

5. Obstacles and Things to Think About:

Although integrated livestock management and sustainable animal husbandry have many advantages, some obstacles must be overcome to be successfully implemented.

Managing the Production of Crops and Animals:

Crop and animal production need to be balanced in integrated systems. While using too much agricultural waste for animal feed may adversely affect soil fertility, overgrazing may cause soil deterioration. To maximize these qualities without sacrificing sustainability, careful planning is needed.

Access to markets and education of consumers:

Finding markets for animal products that are produced responsibly might be difficult. Furthermore, educating consumers to promote awareness of the advantages of goods derived from ethically maintained animals is essential. Increasing demand for these items requires raising awareness of the value of promoting sustainable practices.

The accessibility of land and zoning laws:

Zoning laws and land availability might be obstacles to integrated livestock management. There can be limitations on where animals can be raised or grazed in certain localities. To maximize land usage and guarantee compliance, farmers must manage various rules.

Disease Control:

Prevention is the major focus of sustainable livestock operations, while disease control is still an issue. Resilience is enhanced by tactics like rotational grazing and keeping a variety of breeds, but possible outbreaks must be prevented and controlled with caution.

Financial Suitability:

The long-term success of sustainable animal husbandry depends on ensuring its economic sustainability. Farmers need to weigh the advantages and disadvantages of integrated systems, considering upfront expenditures, continuing upkeep, and possible revenue diversification.

To sum up, integrated livestock management and animal husbandry are essential components of sustainable agriculture that promote a mutually beneficial link between agriculture and animal welfare. Fundamental ideas that support holistic and regenerative agricultural methods include nutrient cycling, rotational grazing, and ethical treatment. Despite its difficulties, sustainable animal husbandry has advantages for the environment, the economy, and the creation of high-quality, ethically produced goods. These advantages go beyond the farm. Building robust and ecologically sensitive food production systems requires integrating livestock into sustainable agricultural systems, which farmers are gradually adopting and improving.

4.5 Composting and Soil Health

In sustainable agriculture, composting is a long-standing and respected method that offers a potent and organic means of improving soil fertility, health, and ecosystem vitality overall. This section explores the fundamentals and advantages of composting, showing how the conversion of organic waste into nutrient-rich humus supports resilient ecosystems and sustainable agriculture.

1. Fundamentals of Composting:

Transformation of Organic Matter:

Fundamentally, composting is the process by which organic waste breaks down biologically to create a nutrient-rich soil conditioner. Microorganisms, including bacteria, fungi, and other decomposers, break down plant and animal components in this process. An aerobic (rich in oxygen) atmosphere is created during composting, which encourages the activity of healthy bacteria.

The ratio of Carbon to Nitrogen (C: N):

Achieving the proper nitrogen and carbon balance is essential to a successful compost. The rate and effectiveness of decomposition are influenced by the carbon-nitrogen ratio, or C: N ratio. A common rule of thumb is to strive for a C: N ratio of 25–30 parts carbon to 1 part nitrogen. This will provide an ideal environment for microbes to break down organic molecules.

Carbon Sources: Materials high in carbon include straw, cardboard, dried leaves, and wood chips.

Sources of Nitrogen: Manure, fresh green leaves, and green plant debris (such as kitchen leftovers) are high in nitrogen.

Aerobic Circumstances

Composting is most successful when enough oxygen is available to support aerobic bacteria's action. To foster an atmosphere favorable to aerobic decomposition, it is essential to turn the compost often, ensure enough aeration is provided, and keep the structure flexible.

Moisture Control:

Retaining the proper moisture content is essential for successful composting. The environment needed for the composting process must be wet, like a wrung-out sponge. Sufficient moisture guarantees the growth of microorganisms and speeds up the decomposition of organic materials. Conversely, too much moisture may cause anaerobic conditions and bad smells.

Temperature Management:

As microorganisms break down organic waste during composting, heat is produced. Temperature is important to monitor and regulate since it affects the kinds of bacteria present and how quickly they decompose. Thermophilic (heat-loving) bacteria dominate the early, high-temperature phase, whereas mesophilic microbes dominate the later, colder phases.

2. The Advantages of Composting

Enrichment of Soil:

As a powerful soil additive, compost enriches soil with vital nutrients. Composting delivers nutrients in a form that plants may easily absorb when the organic waste breaks down. This humus, which is rich in nutrients, enhances soil fertility, structure, and water retention.

Improved Soil Architecture:

Compost encourages the creation of stable aggregates, which strengthens the structure of the soil. These aggregates improve water infiltration and aeration by generating pore spaces in the soil. Better soil structure promotes the development of a healthy soil microbiota, root growth, and nutrient flow.

Drainage and Retention of Water:

Compost's organic matter functions as a sponge to improve the soil's ability to retain and drain water. Compost slows down the drainage rate in sandy soils by helping to hold onto water. It facilitates drainage in clayey soils by allowing surplus water to percolate through the soil profile and reducing compaction.

Diversity of Microbes:

A wide variety of helpful microorganisms are introduced to the soil via compost. Compost contains a variety of microorganisms, including fungi and bacteria, that support the development of a healthy soil microbiome. A healthy microbial population improves soil health overall, suppressing illness and enhancing nutrient cycling.

Decreased Erosion of Soil:

Compost binds soil particles together, reducing soil erosion. Because of the increased soil structure, erosion and nutrient loss are prevented, particularly during periods of severe rainfall. This erosion control works especially well in places that are susceptible or sloping.

Disease Inhibition:

The introduction of a diversified microbial population and certain compost components help control illness in the soil. It has been shown that compost suppresses several soil-borne pathogens, lowering the chance of plant illnesses and encouraging a better harvest.

Sequestration of Carbon:

Carbon sequestration is the process of removing carbon dioxide from the atmosphere and storing it in the soil, and composting is a part of it. As a long-term carbon store and climate change mitigant, compost's stable organic matter adds to soil organic carbon.

Waste Mitigation:

Managing organic waste may be accomplished effectively by composting. Composting lowers the amount of methane—a strong greenhouse gas connected to anaerobic decomposition in landfills—produced by removing yard trash, kitchen scraps, and other organic items from landfills.

3. Compost Types:

The vermicompost

Earthworms are used in vermicomposting, a process that breaks down organic materials. Earthworms eat organic material, break it down, and then release castings that are rich in nutrients. This process produces vermicompost, a very useful kind of compost. This kind of compost works well for small-scale or indoor composting since it is very high in healthy bacteria.

Compost based on manure:

Manure-based compost is created by combining animal dung with other organic compost materials. Manure that has been properly composted removes pathogens and weed seeds, making it an excellent soil supplement. When used sparingly, compost made of manure has a high nutritional content and may improve soil fertility.

Composting Green Waste:

The main ingredients of green waste compost are plant materials, including leaves, grass clippings, and prunings. This compost is a great way to get organic matter and nitrogen. Green waste compost may be used as a nutrient-rich amendment for various crops when properly decomposed.

Localized Composting:

Several towns compost large-scale organic waste collection from homes and businesses. When properly maintained, municipal compost may be useful for regional farming. Nonetheless, to ensure municipal compost is appropriate for a certain crop, keeping an eye on its composition and quality is crucial.

4. Obstacles and Things to Think About:

Composting has many advantages, but to be used successfully, farmers and composters must solve a few issues and concerns.

Problems with Contamination:

There is a chance of contamination, particularly in municipal compost, where different materials are gathered. The presence of contaminants like plastic, glass, or persistent pesticides may have a detrimental effect on the compost's quality.

Odor Control:

Improper management of composting might result in smells that bother neighbors. Odors may be reduced with enough aeration, careful moisture control, and consideration of the carbon-nitrogen ratio.

Growing Up:

Careful planning is needed when expanding composting facilities to accommodate bigger farms or towns. It is necessary to consider variables, including feedstock availability, space needs, and equipment issues.

Outreach in Education:

It is crucial to educate and raise public understanding of appropriate composting techniques. Many people and communities may be unaware of the fundamentals of composting or its advantages. Outreach initiatives may help close this gap.

Observation and Examination:

Regular testing and monitoring are essential to guarantee compost's efficacy as a soil additive. This entails evaluating the concentrations of nutrients, microbiological activity, and possible pollutants. Farmers have to evaluate compost proactively before applying it widely.

To sum up, composting is an essential component of sustainable agriculture and provides a safe, efficient way to improve the fertility and health of the soil. The development of nutrient-rich humus that helps plants and the larger environment is made possible by the principles of composting, which include the transformation of organic waste, aerobic conditions, and balanced C: N ratios. The many varieties of compost, ranging from municipal to vermicompost, provide adaptability for various settings and sizes. Notwithstanding its difficulties, composting helps create resilient and sustainable food production systems, reduce waste, and preserve the environment, in addition to helping individual farms. Building regenerative and ecologically sound agricultural systems requires compost, which is becoming increasingly important in sustainable agriculture as farmers, gardeners, and communities adopt and improve composting techniques.

Chapter 5: Off-Grid Living

5.1 Harnessing Renewable Energy Sources

The deliberate use of renewable energy sources becomes a critical component in the quest for sustainable living, especially when considering off-grid life. This section explores the ideas, methods, and advantages of using renewable energy to power homesteads. It summarizes how renewable energy sources may promote self-sufficiency and lessen environmental impact.

1. **Renewable Energy Principles:**

Non-renewable vs renewable:

Naturally renewing resources, including sunshine, wind, rain, tides, and geothermal heat, are the source of renewable energy. Renewable energy uses the Earth's natural processes to provide electricity without depleting limited resources, unlike non-renewable sources like fossil fuels. This difference emphasizes how renewable energy solutions are long-term viable and sustainable.

Inconsistency and Holding:

The erratic nature of renewable energy sources is a major drawback. There are times when the wind blows and times when the sun shines. Effective storage options, such as batteries, are essential for overcoming this. When renewable energy output is low, extra energy created during peak circumstances may be captured and stored thanks to battery technology.

Decentralized Generation of Power:

In contrast to the centralized approach associated with traditional energy sources, renewable energy encourages decentralized power production. By enabling people and communities to generate energy, decentralization lessens reliance on expansive power systems and minimizes transmission losses.

2. Renewable Energy Types:

Solar Power:

Solar energy uses photovoltaic (PV) cells to capture sunlight and turn it into electrical power. For usage in houses, these cells convert sunlight into direct current (DC), which is then converted into alternating current (AC). Sunlight is captured by solar panels placed on roofs or in open areas, making solar energy a flexible and extensively available renewable resource.

Wind Power:

Wind energy uses wind turbines to transform the kinetic energy of the wind into electrical energy. A generator uses the wind's rotational energy to create electrical power while the turbine's blades spin. Wind turbines facilitate the increasing dependence on wind energy, whether large-scale community projects or small-scale personal use units.

Water-powered:

Using the energy of falling or flowing water, hydropower produces electricity. While run-of-river and micro-hydro systems, new innovations, serve smaller-scale applications, traditional hydropower systems use dams and rivers. Water's gravitational force makes hydropower a dependable and sustainable energy source.

Thermogenic Energy:

Geothermal energy generates electricity by harnessing the heat that exists inside the Earth. Geothermal power plants use heat below the Earth's surface to create steam, which powers turbines linked to generators. This consistent and dependable energy source is especially available in areas with much geothermal activity.

Biological Energy:

Biomass energy generates heat or power using organic resources like wood, agricultural remnants, and animal manure. Biomass may be immediately burnt to provide heat or processed to make biofuels. Although carbon dioxide is released during biomass burning, the total effect is thought to be carbon-neutral since the plants that were eaten during growth absorbed carbon dioxide from the atmosphere.

3. Advantages of Using Sustainable Energy:

Sustainability of the Environment:

The favorable effects of renewable energy on the environment are among its main advantages. Renewable energy sources emit little or no greenhouse gasses, in contrast to fossil fuels that contribute to climate change. Renewable energy sources like solar, wind, and other energy may lessen the environmental impact of energy use.

Independence in Energy:

Because renewable energy generates electricity in a decentralized manner, it helps achieve energy independence. Renewable energy homesteads are less dependent on centralized power systems and, therefore, more susceptible to outages. This independence improves resilience and self-sufficiency and is especially useful in isolated locations or during crises.

Cost Reductions:

Although there may be a high upfront cost associated with renewable energy systems, there are significant long-term cost benefits. The cost of solar panels has steadily decreased, while wind turbine efficiency is still rising. Furthermore, renewable sources are financially appealing throughout the systems' lives due to the lack of continuous fuel expenses.

Local economies and the creation of jobs:

The industry for renewable energy is becoming a major employer. Local economies benefit from installing, upkeep, and producing renewable energy system components. Opportunities for employment and economic growth increase with the demand for renewable technology.

Diminished Ecological Effects:

Using renewable energy reduces greenhouse gas emissions and the environmental damage caused by fossil fuel extraction, transportation, and combustion. It reduces the harmful effects of resource exploitation, protects ecosystems, and lowers air and water pollution.

4. Technologies for Utilizing Renewable Energy:

Photovoltaic (PV) Systems in the Sun:

Solar PV systems use solar panels to generate power from sunlight. These systems may be off-grid with battery storage for self-sufficiency or grid-tied, enabling surplus energy to be channeled back into the system. Innovations like solar shingles and transparent solar cells built into windows result from advancements in solar technology.

Wind Generators:

Wind energy is captured by wind turbines, which come in various sizes, from giant industrial to tiny domestic. Both horizontal- and vertical-axis designs are used to harness wind energy, and turbine efficiency improvements keep wind power growing.

Systems Hydroelectric:

The size of hydropower systems varies, ranging from massive dams to tiny micro-hydro facilities. Electrical energy is produced by harnessing the kinetic energy of falling or flowing water. Another hydroelectric method, pumped hydro storage, stores extra energy by pumping water to a higher altitude with extra electricity, which is then used to generate power later.

Pumps for geothermal heat:

For heating and cooling buildings, geothermal heat pumps use the steady temperature found under the surface of the Earth. These systems provide effective temperature management by moving heat to or from the Earth, which lessens the need for conventional heating and cooling techniques.

Systems for Biomass Energy:

Technologies such as anaerobic digesters, gasifiers, and biomass boilers are examples of biomass energy systems. Anaerobic digesters break down organic waste to create biogas, gasifiers transform biomass into a gaseous fuel, and biomass boilers burn organic materials for heat. These technologies cover various applications, including industrial operations and home heating.

5. Obstacles and Things to Think About:

Challenges with Intermittency and Storage:

Consistently satisfying energy needs is challenging since some renewable sources are intermittent. Wind speeds may fluctuate, and solar power is affected on cloudy days. To meet these difficulties, we need dependable storage options, such as cutting-edge battery technology.

The initial outlay and affordability:

Even though there are substantial long-term cost benefits, some people or groups may find the initial investment in renewable energy systems prohibitive. Promoting affordability and accessibility via policies and financial incentives is essential for hastening the adoption of renewable technology.

Land Use and Visual Appeal:

For example, large-scale solar or wind farms need a significant amount of land to be used. It is crucial to strike a balance between the demand for clean energy and issues related to land use and aesthetics, particularly in highly inhabited or ecologically sensitive places.

Geographic Restrictions and Resource Availability:

There are regional differences in the accessibility of renewable resources. Windy regions are more suitable for wind power, whereas places with plenty of sunshine may have easier access to solar energy. Developing creative methods or combining various technologies may be necessary to overcome these geographical constraints.

Technological Integration and Advancements:

Further technical developments are required to improve the integration and efficiency of renewable energy systems. To further maximize the production of renewable energy, research and development efforts are being made to create innovative storage solutions, boost the efficiency of wind turbines, and enhance the performance of solar panels.

In summary, renewable energy sources are essential to attaining off-grid, sustainable living. The wide range of renewable technologies, which include hydropower, geothermal, wind, and solar, enable people and communities to generate clean energy, promoting resilience and environmental responsibility. Beyond only lowering greenhouse gas emissions, renewable energy offers cost savings, job development, and energy independence. Integrating renewable energy into off-grid life becomes not only a goal but a realistic and significant way to shape a sustainable and self-sufficient future as technology continues to advance and solve problems.

5.2 Water Conservation and Harvesting

Water—a valuable and limited resource—takes center stage in the quest for sustainable living, particularly in off-grid situations. To lessen dependency on outside water sources, homesteads should practice responsible water management, as this section explains the fundamentals, practices, and advantages of water collection and conservation.

❖ **Water Conservation Principles:**

Knowing About Water Scarcity

Water conservation is very important, as shown by the water shortage that is being made worse by climate change and population expansion. A change toward responsible water usage is required because water supplies are limited, and the water demand is rising. This entails implementing procedures that reduce waste, prioritize effectiveness, and guarantee the sustainability of water supplies.

Effective Use of Water:

Efficient water usage aims to maximize the amount of water used for anything from domestic to agriculture. Reducing total water demand may be achieved by implementing water-efficient technology, such as smart irrigation systems, high-efficiency appliances, and low-flow faucets. This idea applies to everyday activities and agricultural methods, including the usage of water inside and outdoors.

Both Xeriscaping and Landscaping:

Strategic methods for water conservation in outdoor environments include landscaping and xeriscaping. The need for excessive watering is reduced by using xeriscaping techniques, such as mulching and grouping plants with comparable water requirements and native, drought-resistant species in landscaping. These methods encourage water efficiency while producing visually beautiful landscapes.

Water from the Rain:

The foundation of water conservation is seeing rainfall as a beneficial resource rather than an annoyance. Rainwater harvesting lessens the demand for nearby water resources and lessens dependency on outside water sources for various purposes, including domestic chores and irrigation. Simple rain buckets to intricate cisterns and storage tanks are examples of rainwater collection systems.

❖ **Techniques for Gathering Water:**

Rainfall Gathering:

Gathering and preserving rainwater for future use is known as rainwater harvesting. This technique collects rainwater from roofs, gutters, and other surfaces and is directed into storage bins. More complex solutions incorporate filtering systems and sizable storage tanks, while simpler systems often only link downspouts to barrels. Rainwater collection may be used for various tasks, such as supplemental home watering and garden irrigation.

Systems for Greywater:

Greywater systems reuse water from dishwashing, laundry, and bathing for uses other than potable water. Utilizing greywater for landscape irrigation or gardening lessens the need for freshwater resources. Greywater systems range from simple ones that divert water directly to plants to more complex ones that include filter and treatment elements.

Harvesting runoff:

Runoff harvesting is collecting and using water runoff from surfaces such as patios, driveways, and roadways. This strategy directs runoff to storage systems or specified regions rather than letting it flow away. Porous surfaces, like gravel or permeable pavers, allow water to seep into the soil, lowering runoff and encouraging groundwater replenishment.

Using fog nets and collecting dew:

Fog nets and dew harvesting are creative methods to collect water from the air in specific humid climates. While dew harvesting is gathering water that condenses on surfaces overnight, fog nets are mesh structures that catch water droplets from fog. These techniques show how water harvesting may be adjusted to various environmental situations, albeit more specialized.

❖ **Advantages of Harvesting and Conserving Water:**

Decreased Demand on Local Water Resources:

Water harvesting and conservation ease the burden on regional water resources, especially in locations where water is scarce. Homesteads help manage water resources sustainably so that they are available to current and future generations by lowering dependency on centralized water sources like wells or municipal water systems.

Enhanced Adaptability During Dry Conditions:

Conservation and collection of water improves resilience during dry spells in areas vulnerable to drought or water constraints. Water shortages are lessened when one has access to stored rainwater, recovered greywater, or other harvested sources. This guarantees that there will always be water available for necessities.

Eco-friendly Landscaping Techniques:

Water-saving techniques like xeriscaping and effective watering aid sustainable landscaping. Water-efficient landscape design not only preserves biodiversity, improves soil quality and maintains the general balance of the ecosystem.

Cost Reductions:

Water bills and infrastructure maintenance expenses are reduced when conservation measures are implemented. Rainwater collecting eliminates the need to buy water or make costly investments in water infrastructure by offering a plentiful and free water supply for various applications.

Reduction of Stormwater Problems:

Stormwater management is aided by techniques for gathering water, such as runoff harvesting. These techniques lessen floods, stop soil erosion, and assist in replenishing groundwater aquifers by catching and managing runoff. This all-encompassing strategy tackles the problems of stormwater management and water shortages.

❖ **Water Harvesting Technologies:**

Cisterns and Rain Barrels:

Cisterns and rain barrels are key components of rainwater gathering systems. Rainwater from rooftops is collected and stored in these containers, giving you access to non-potable needs like gardening and irrigation. Larger storage capacity for more extensive water harvesting requirements is provided by cisterns, which come in various sizes.

Systems for Diverting Greywater:

Greywater diversion systems collect and divert water used for domestic tasks outside. Simple pipe diversion systems to more complex configurations with filters and distribution networks are examples of these systems. Water that would otherwise go down the drain may be efficiently reused thanks to greywater diversion.

Surfaces that Permeate:

Water may seep into the soil via porous surfaces, such as gravel or permeable pavers, aiding runoff collection. By lowering the quantity of water that runs off impervious surfaces, these surfaces minimize surface runoff and encourage groundwater recharge.

Cloud Nets:

Fog nets are buildings with mesh materials that catch water droplets from fog in areas where fog is common. Water droplets condense and gather as the fog moves through the mesh, offering a novel way to extract water from the atmosphere.

Systems for Harvesting Dew:

Systems for collecting dew use surfaces that promote the condensation of atmospheric water vapor. These surfaces collect Condensed water, often made to promote dew production and may subsequently be directed into storage bins. Even though it's less prevalent, dew collecting shows how versatile water-gathering technology may be.

❖ **Obstacles and Things to Think About:**

Treatment and Quality:

For its intended use, gathered water must be of a certain purity. Water may need to be treated to satisfy specific requirements, depending on the source and harvesting technique. Processes, including sedimentation, disinfection, and filtering, could be required to deal with possible pathogens and pollutants.

Regulation and Zoning Factors:

Zoning laws and local ordinances may impact the installation of water harvesting systems. Water harvesting may be subject to additional regulations or licenses in certain places, particularly if it entails changing landscapes or existing buildings. Adherence to regional laws is necessary to prevent legal complications.

Upkeep and System Durability:

Water harvesting devices, such as cisterns or rain barrels, need to be maintained regularly to preserve their durability and usefulness. Regular maintenance that keeps the system functioning well includes cleaning the gutters, examining storage containers, and testing the filters. System failures, pollution, and blockages may all be avoided with routine maintenance.

Dimensions and Style:

Water harvesting system dimensions and design are important factors to take into account. Considerations including roof area, rainfall patterns, and water consumption must be made to choose the right storage containers or harvesting system capacity. Well-designed systems maximize the efficiency of water collection and storage.

Outreach in Education:

For broad adoption, raising awareness and educating on water harvesting and conservation is essential—Many of these activities' advantages and guiding principles. Outreach educational initiatives may encourage a shared commitment to responsible water management by empowering communities to conserve water.

Water collection and conservation are essential aspects of off-grid life that provide long-term answers to water shortages and encourage wise water use. These techniques, which range from collecting rainfall to reusing gray water, enable homesteads to lessen their reliance on outside water sources, increase their resistance to drought, and support the sustainable use of water resources. The advantages go beyond individual homesteads and include financial savings, stormwater problem reduction, and encouraging environmentally friendly landscaping techniques. Incorporating water harvesting and conservation becomes not only a practical need but also a responsible decision in creating a sustainable and water-resilient future as awareness and technology advance.

5.3 Building Off-Grid Structures

Off-grid living encompasses more than just sustainable water and energy techniques; it also affects our buildings. The concepts, procedures, and advantages of constructing off-grid buildings are covered in detail in this section. Sustainable living is based on building self-sufficient and environmentally friendly homes, which involves careful planning and execution of construction methods.

❖ **Off-Grid Construction Principles:**

Flexibility and Self-Sufficiency:

Building off the grid is based on the core principles of independence and self-sufficiency. The objective of these buildings is to function independently, reducing dependence on outside resources like waste management systems, water supply, and municipal electricity. Building off the grid aims to build houses that can gather their water, produce their electricity, and handle their trash.

Integration of the Environment:

Off-grid buildings are thoughtfully constructed to integrate the environment. By blending in with the natural environment, the aim is to reduce the ecological imprint. This might include selecting locally produced and sustainable construction materials and designing structures that blend in with the environment rather than compete with it.

Efficiency of Resources:

One of the main principles of off-grid building is resource efficiency. This philosophy emphasizes using resources as efficiently as possible, cutting waste, and using reused or repurposed materials. Off-grid constructions aim to use resources as efficiently as possible from the ground up, which promotes more environmentally friendly building practices.

Durability and Resilience:

Resilience and durability are prioritized in off-grid construction to endure the difficulties of isolated life. This covers factors including long-term wear, seismic activity, and harsh weather. The aim is to build houses with minimum upkeep and repairs over time, survive and flourish in their particular environmental situation.

❖ **Off-Grid Construction Techniques:**

The Design of Passive Solar:

A key component of off-grid building is passive solar architecture, which uses the sun's energy to heat, cool, and light a space without mechanical equipment. This design strategy maximizes solar gain in the winter and minimizes it in the summer by considering elements including building direction, window location, and thermal mass. The building's interior comfort and energy efficiency are improved via passive solar architecture.

Energy-Conscious Building Exterior:

The three main components of an energy-efficient building envelope are thermal mass, airtightness, and insulation. Temperature stability results from well-insulated floors, walls, and roofs, which lowers the need for intense heating or cooling. Reducing heat loss via airtight construction is combined with regulating interior temperature through thermal mass materials like rammed earth or adobe.

Disconnected Energy Systems:

To satisfy their power demands, off-grid constructions combine autonomous energy systems. This might include small-scale hydropower plants, wind turbines, and solar panels. Battery storage is essential for a consistent and dependable power supply during low-energy generation.

Organic and Regional Construction Materials:

Selecting natural and locally available building materials in off-grid construction is a sustainable strategy. Reclaimed wood, adobe, cob, straw bales, and other materials reduce the environmental effect of extraction and shipping. Utilizing plentiful resources in the surrounding area increases resource efficiency and lowers overall carbon emissions.

Using Rainwater Harvesting in Building:

It is possible to use off-grid ideas throughout the building process. Rainwater harvesting systems may gather water for construction, such as supplying water to workers on the job site or mixing concrete. By using this method, there is less need to use outside water sources during construction.

Managing Waste: Strategies

Waste management techniques are included in off-grid construction to reduce the environmental effect of building operations. This includes appropriately disposing of non-recyclable garbage, recycling building debris, and composting organic elements. The aim is to design buildings with the least possible ecological impact during construction.

❖ **Advantages of Building Off-Grid:**

Independence in Energy:

Energy independence is a major advantage of off-grid buildings. Off-grid buildings are less susceptible to outages in centralized power systems since they generate electricity from renewable sources. This independence is especially useful in isolated areas where connecting to the grid can be expensive or impracticable.

Lesser Impact on the Environment:

Off-grid building reduces its environmental effect by using locally and sustainably produced materials. The building process has minimal carbon impact using eco-friendly procedures and reducing dependency on outside resources. This is consistent with the more general objectives of ecological care and environmental protection.

Savings on Overhead:

The off-grid building may have equivalent or higher initial costs than conventional construction. Still, there are substantial long-term cost reductions. Cheaper continuous costs, such as cheaper energy bills and less maintenance needs, are a result of resource efficiency, renewable energy systems, and energy-efficient designs.

Adaptability to Outside Influences:

Off-grid buildings are, by nature, more resistant to outside influences, such as interruptions in the water supply and power outages. A certain level of self-sufficiency is ensured by integrating independent water and electricity systems, enabling residents to withstand unanticipated outages in municipal services or bad weather.

Relationship to Nature:

Building off the grid often places a high value on being close to nature. These buildings are intended to improve the residents' relationship with the surrounding environment, whether via passive solar design, letting in natural light or using natural building materials that mix in with the surroundings. This focus on the natural world makes life there healthier and more sustainable.

❖ **Innovations and Technologies in Off-Grid Building:**

Planetships:

With its use of recyclable materials, rainwater collecting, and passive solar architecture, earthships are a noteworthy breakthrough in off-grid buildings. These self-sufficient homes integrate environmental integration, energy efficiency, and sustainability into their off-grid architecture.

Living walls and green roofs:

Living walls and green roofs are examples of technology that improve a building's environmental performance. Green roofs include:

- We are adding more green areas.

- They are lowering stormwater runoff.

- We are providing insulation.

- Growing flora on the roof's surface.

Vertical gardens, often known as living walls, support biodiversity while improving interior air quality and aesthetic appeal.

Modular & Prefab Building:

Modular and prefab building techniques provide effective and adaptable off-grid options. Construction time and waste are decreased using prefabricated components made off-site and installed on-site. Buildings with modular components may be expanded and adjustable, making them suitable for a range of off-grid living situations.

Intelligent Home Technology:

Smart home technology can maximize energy efficiency and improve comfort in off-grid buildings. To improve overall energy efficiency and sustainability, homeowners may monitor and manage their energy use with the help of energy-efficient appliances, smart thermostats, and home automation systems.

Novelties in Eco-Friendly Materials:

The off-grid building is progressing because of ongoing advancements in sustainable materials. This covers creating materials with enhanced insulating qualities, a high percentage of recycled content, and little environmental effect. Sustainable material innovations seek to improve building practices regarding environmental impact and performance.

❖ **Obstacles and Things to Think About:**

Zoning and regulatory challenges:

Zoning and regulatory issues may arise during off-grid development since building laws and regulations are often created for conventional constructions linked to centralized services. To overcome these obstacles, it could be necessary to collaborate with local authorities to create regulations that respect off-grid ideas while guaranteeing compliance and safety.

Requirements for Knowledge and Skills:

The off-grid building needs unique knowledge and abilities to be implemented successfully. Architects, builders, and other construction industry professionals should know about sustainable building techniques, renewable energy systems, and passive solar design. Professional education and training in these domains are necessary to accept off-grid buildings.

Initial Expenses and Funding:

Off-grid buildings may save money in the long run, but some people or communities may find the upfront expenses prohibitive. Reaching out to financial organizations who comprehend the long-term advantages or looking into alternate funding sources may be necessary to get finance that values sustainable and off-grid qualities.

Maintenance and system observation:

Off-grid buildings with sustainable elements and renewable energy systems need constant upkeep and observation. For best results, it's important to regularly inspect water systems, solar panels, batteries, and other parts. Occupants must possess knowledge of the necessary maintenance and have dependable help available to them when required.

Ability to Adjust to Local Climates:

It's critical to design off-grid buildings that can adjust to the environment where they are located. Off-grid building effectiveness and efficiency are enhanced by considering climate-specific factors, from insulation selection to energy system size. The need to customize designs to particular environmental situations is highlighted by the possibility that a one-size-fits-all strategy may not be appropriate.

To sum up, creating off-grid homes embodies a comprehensive strategy for sustainable living that includes the ideas of resource efficiency, environmental integration, and self-sufficiency. Off-grid houses actively promote ecological resilience while minimizing environmental effects by incorporating renewable energy sources and designing with passive solar energy. Beyond energy and financial savings, the advantages include:

- Improved resistance to outside influences.

- A closer relationship with the natural world.

- Advancements in sustainable technology.

Off-grid buildings can completely change how we live and create, promoting more sustainable and peaceful coexistence with the environment as the sector develops.

Here's a text-based outline/table summarizing the key points for the topic "5.3 Building Off-Grid Structures":

Principles of Off-Grid Construction	Methods of Off-Grid Construction	Benefits of Off-Grid Construction	Technologies and Innovations	Challenges and Considerations
- Self-Sufficiency and Independence	- Passive Solar Design	- Energy Independence	- Earthships	- Regulatory and Zoning Challenges

- Environmental Integration	- Energy-Efficient Building Envelope	- Lower Environmental Impact	- Green Roofs and Living Walls	- Skills and Knowledge Requirements
- Resource Efficiency	- Off-Grid Energy Systems	- Cost Savings Over Time	- Prefab and Modular Construction	- Upfront Costs and Financing
- Resilience and Durability	- Natural and Local Building Materials	- Resilience to External Factors	- Smart Home Technologies	- Maintenance and System Monitoring
	- Rainwater Harvesting for Construction	- Connection with Nature	- Innovations in Sustainable Materials	- Adaptability to Local Climates

This table provides a structured overview of the key aspects related to building off-grid structures, including the principles, methods, benefits, technologies, and challenges associated with this sustainable living approach.

5.4 Waste Reduction and Recycling

Reducing garbage and recycling are essential in encouraging ecologically sensitive and sustainable lives when pursuing off-grid living. This section goes into the ideas, techniques, and advantages of trash reduction and recycling procedures within the context of off-grid life. These tactics, which range from reducing waste production to reusing resources novelly, are designed to lessen their negative effects on the environment while fostering self-sufficiency.

❖ **The fundamentals of waste reduction**

Cutting Down on Consumption:

The idea of reducing consumption is at the heart of off-grid trash reduction. This entails making deliberate and conscientious decisions about purchasing and consumption habits. Off-grid residents often value quality more than quantity, choosing sturdy, long-lasting objects to reduce the need for disposal and replacements.

Steer clear of single-use items:

One of the most important concepts in waste reduction is avoiding single-use goods. Off-grid people try to choose reusable alternatives because they understand the negative effects of single-use items on the environment. This also applies to reusable alternatives for food containers, water bottles, and shopping bags, which significantly reduce trash production.

Putting Organic Waste to Bed:

An essential element of waste reduction is composting organic waste, especially in off-grid environments with few choices for garbage disposal. Off-grid residents use composting systems to turn yard trash, food scraps, and other organic wastes into nutrient-rich compost. By doing this, organic waste is kept out of landfills and useful soil nutrients for farming and gardening are created.

Repurposing and Upcycling:

Repurposing and upcycling include giving unwanted or abandoned objects a new lease on life. Off-grid folks frequently display innovation in reusing resources, converting old pallets into furniture, altering glass jars into storage containers, or utilizing waste wood for different building projects. This method gives off-grid living areas a distinctive, individualized touch while cutting down on trash.

Careful Selection of Packaging:

Making thoughtful packaging decisions helps reduce waste by prioritizing goods with minimum or environmentally friendly packaging. Off-grid customers may choose items using biodegradable or recyclable packaging materials and, in certain situations, opt for bulk purchases to limit the total package trash created.

❖ Waste Reduction and Recycling Techniques:

Sorting and Separating Sources:

Sorting and source separation are the first steps toward effective trash reduction and recycling. Off-grid dwellers set aside specific bins for organic garbage, recyclables, and non-recyclables, among other waste categories. By following this procedure, recycling is streamlined, and items are routed to composting or recycling correctly.

Community-Based Recycling Programs:

In off-grid areas, collaborative efforts frequently lead to the formation of community recycling projects. Shared recycling programs and stations make it easier for things to be disposed of and recycled properly, which promotes a group effort to reduce waste. Additionally, this strategy encourages knowledge and instruction on recycling procedures.

DIY Recycling Projects:

Do-it-yourself (DIY) recycling initiatives are one practical way off-grid residents use their hands. This might entail manufacturing useful objects from wasted materials, such as weaving carpets from old fabric scraps or developing storage solutions from reused containers. In addition to cutting trash, do-it-yourself recycling initiatives promote a resourceful and independent lifestyle.

Using Recycled Materials in Construction:

In off-grid buildings, integrating recycled materials is a frequent technique. Off-grid builders ingeniously use recycled materials in their projects, from refurbishing old windows and doors to creating buildings out of salvaged wood. This lessens the need for new materials and gives the built environment more personality and individuality.

Transportable Recycling Options:

There may not be easy access to official recycling facilities in isolated off-grid areas. As a result, some off-grid households and communities use mobile recycling systems. This may include bringing recyclables to local recycling facilities regularly or working with mobile recycling services that go to outlying locations.

❖ **Advantages of Recycling and Waste Reduction:**

Preservation of the Environment:

The fundamental advantage of trash reduction and recycling in off-grid life is environmental conservation. Off-grid people help to preserve ecosystems, reduce greenhouse gas emissions, and conserve natural resources by encouraging recycling and decreasing garbage transported to landfills. This fits in with the overarching objective of reducing the negative effects of human activity on the environment.

Efficiency and Conservation of Resources:

Recycling and waste minimization help to save resources and increase productivity. By lowering the need for new raw materials, recycling and material reuse help save the energy and resources needed for extraction and manufacture. This strategy supports a circular economy where resources are fully recycled and reused, which aligns with sustainability ideals.

Cost Reductions:

Reducing garbage and recycling may save a lot of money while living off the grid, especially when resources are few. Off-grid folks lower their total expenditures by recycling materials, repurposing products, and limiting needless purchases. This economic effectiveness is consistent with the off-grid lifestyle's self-sufficiency philosophy.

Building Communities and Working Together:

Waste reduction and recycling programs often promote cooperation and community development in off-grid environments. Collaborative recycling initiatives foster shared accountability, promote collaboration among neighbors, and provide avenues for information sharing. Beyond trash reduction, this collaborative mentality permeates all facets of sustainable living.

Creative and Aesthetic Expression:

Reusing and upcycling materials promotes creative and aesthetic expression while reducing waste. Off-grid residents often enjoy repurposing materials to create useful and aesthetically pleasing objects that give their homes a distinctive flair. This creative element adds to a feeling of personality and improves the lifestyle as a whole.

❖ **Waste Reduction Innovations and Technologies:**

Tools and Apps for Precycling:

Apps and tools for recycling help those living off the grid make wise purchases. With the help of these resources, customers may make decisions regarding items that will produce the least amount of trash by learning about product packaging, recycling possibilities, and ecologically appropriate substitutes.

Systems for Compact Waste Management:

Compact waste management system innovations provide effective waste processing options, supporting off-grid living. These technologies provide off-grid residents with more alternatives for managing their garbage responsibly. Examples of these systems include small-scale recycling equipment, compact composting units, and creative methods for on-site waste management.

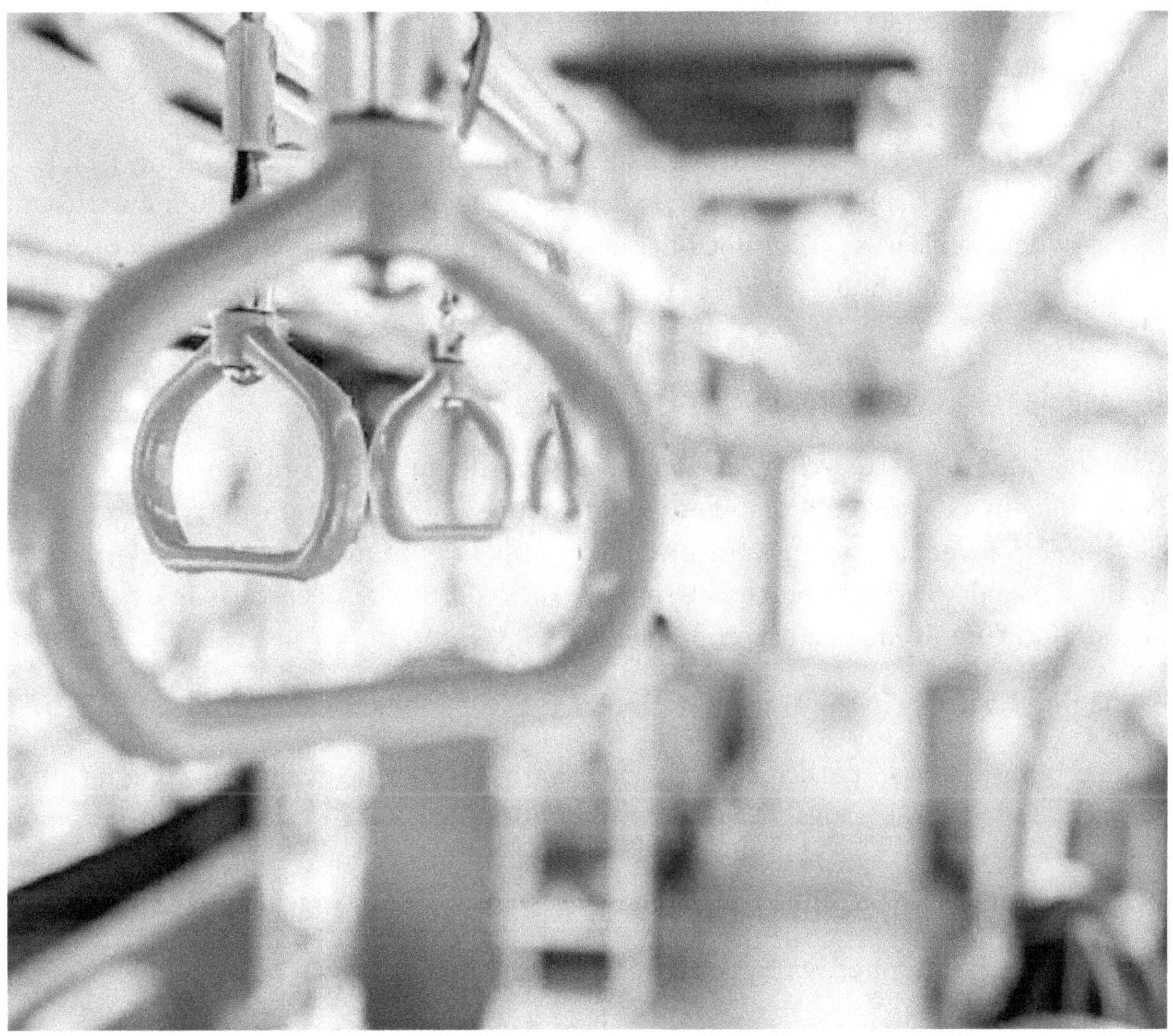

Platforms for Recycling in Communities:

As tools for off-grid communities, digital platforms and applications that support neighborhood-based recycling programs are starting to appear. These platforms foster interpersonal connections, disseminate information about recycling options, and organize neighborhood-wide material collection and recycling initiatives. This technical breakthrough boosts the efficacy of trash reduction activities in off-grid areas.

Sustainable Packaging Options:

Advancements in eco-friendly packaging solutions assist in waste reduction by encouraging biodegradable, compostable, or readily recyclable materials. Off-grid customers benefit from these advances by accessing items with packaging that matches their desire to minimize environmental impact.

❖ **Obstacles and Things to Think About:**

Restricted Infrastructure for Recycling:

Off-grid communities may confront issues relating to insufficient recycling facilities. Transporting recyclables to designated sites might be logistically challenging in distant places where official recycling facilities are lacking. Off-grid people must work with neighboring communities or look into other recycling options to overcome these obstacles.

Knowledge of Education:

Initiatives aimed at recycling and reducing trash must succeed partly because of education. In off-grid environments, where access to information may be restricted, developing awareness about the necessity of waste reduction, effective recycling methods, and the environmental impact of consumer decisions is crucial for encouraging involvement and comprehension.

Managing Logistics in the Transportation of Waste:

Transporting garbage, particularly recyclables, from off-grid sites to recycling facilities may create logistical issues. Off-grid communities may need to design transportation solutions depending on periodic visits from mobile recycling services or organizing pooled transportation efforts to overcome these logistical challenges.

Recycle Options Limited for Specific Materials:

Recyclability possibilities for certain materials may be restricted, especially in off-grid areas. Materials not readily recyclable or lacking established recycling pathways may obstruct waste reduction initiatives. Off-grid persons may need to discover inventive alternatives for recycling or reusing such products to limit their environmental effects.

Seasonal Differences in the Production of Waste:

Living off the grid often entails being in tune with the cycles of nature, particularly the seasonal changes. This might result in varying patterns of waste output, with peak periods throughout specific seasons. Managing waste in light of seasonal fluctuation demands adaptable techniques and proactive planning to handle the particular problems of fluctuating trash quantities.

In summary, recycling and trash reduction are:

- Essential elements of the off-grid lifestyle.

- Representing the values of resource efficiency.

- Community cooperation.

- Environmental responsibility.

By following the ideals of decreasing consumption, embracing creative recycling techniques, and adopting new technology, off-grid persons contribute to a sustainable and self-sufficient existence. The advantages extend beyond environmental protection to embrace financial savings, community development, and the creative expression of reusing materials.

Despite constraints associated with restricted infrastructure and logistical concerns, the dedication to waste reduction in off-grid living represents a larger trend toward responsible and thoughtful consumption, supporting a peaceful cohabitation with the natural environment. As technology and understanding continue to improve, trash reduction and recycling will remain important in creating a sustainable future for off-grid settlements.

5.5 Implementing Sustainable Technologies

Regarding off-grid living, using sustainable technology is essential to becoming self-sufficient and maintaining environmental balance. The advantages, strategies, and ideas of incorporating sustainable technology into off-grid living are covered in detail in this section. These technologies enable people and communities to flourish independently while reducing their environmental impact, from using renewable energy sources to implementing eco-friendly advancements.

Using Sources of Renewable Energy:

Solar power is one of the main sustainable technologies used in off-grid living. Solar panels collect sunlight and turn it into power, usually installed on roofs or the ground. Off-grid residents use solar power systems to provide electricity for appliances, lights, and other essentials. Developments in solar technology, such as more effective panels and energy storage options, increase the dependability and efficiency of solar electricity when used off the grid.

Wind Generators:

Another essential part of off-grid renewable energy solutions is wind turbines. Wind energy is captured by properly positioned turbines, which provide power that may be stored in batteries for later use. Wind power may be used as an alternative or supplement to solar electricity in off-grid areas with regular wind patterns. Because of its adaptability, wind turbines enable off-grid populations to generate electricity without direct sunshine.

Systems Hydroelectric:

Hydroelectric systems provide a viable, sustainable energy source in certain off-grid environments with access to running water. The kinetic energy of flowing water is converted into electrical power by small-scale hydroelectric turbines. Hydroelectric systems may be used by off-grid communities located next to rivers or streams to help meet their energy demands. This strategy works especially well for reliable electricity production regardless of the weather.

Integrating Various Energy Sources:

Many off-grid systems use a hybrid strategy combining many renewable energy sources to provide a consistent and dependable power supply. Off-grid residents use hydropower generators, solar panels, and wind turbines to integrate and strengthen their energy systems. Hybrid configurations optimize energy generation and storage, providing a complete answer to the difficulties associated with off-grid life.

❖ **Harvesting and Conserving Water:**

Systems for Harvesting Rainwater:

Living off the grid often means relying on one's resources for water, and rainwater-gathering devices are essential for supplying water demands. Roofs direct rainwater into storage tanks, which may be filtered and kept for domestic activities, drinking, and gardening. Rainwater gathering encourages sustainable water management and lessens reliance on outside water sources.

Effective Irrigation Techniques:

Effective irrigation techniques are crucial in off-grid environments where gardening or agriculture is a component of sustainable living. For example, drip irrigation reduces water waste by giving plants' bases direct access to water. By focusing on this area, water is utilized more effectively, encouraging healthy plant development and protecting this valuable resource.

Methods of Water Purification:

A crucial component of living off the grid is purifying your water, particularly using natural sources like gathered rainwater. Water purification technologies that are environmentally friendly include UV sterilization, filtration systems, and other chemical-free techniques. Off-grid people prioritize dependable and safe water filtration to guarantee that they have access to clean, drinkable water for household purposes.

Preservation Techniques:

Off-grid lives are deeply embedded with water-saving measures. People develop routines that include utilizing low-flow devices, quickly repairing leaks, and recycling greywater for uses other than potable water. Following these guidelines may reduce water use, and appropriate use of this limited resource can be guaranteed.

Eco-Friendly Water Storage Options:

Off-grid residents use sustainable water storage systems to store and manage their water supply more efficiently. Rainwater harvesting is stored for a long time in tanks or cisterns, often constructed from environmentally acceptable materials. Gravity flow is considered in designing and positioning various storage options to help distribute water throughout the living area.

1. **Constructing Off-Grid Buildings:**

The Design of Passive Solar:

Passive solar design is a sustainable building technique that maximizes natural sunshine for lighting and warmth while designing off-grid buildings. Without active heating or cooling systems, a structure may be designed to optimize energy efficiency via window orientation, material selection, and thermal mass considerations.

Energy-Conscious Building Exterior:

The building envelope, which consists of the walls, roof, and floors, is essential for maintaining a pleasant temperature in off-grid buildings. Insulation, airtightness, and thermal mass principles are all included in energy-efficient building envelopes to reduce heat input or loss and lessen the need for external heating or cooling systems.

Disconnected Energy Systems:

To satisfy their power demands, off-grid constructions combine autonomous energy systems. This might include small-scale hydropower plants, wind turbines, and solar panels. Battery storage is essential for a consistent and dependable power supply during low-energy generation.

Organic and Regional Construction Materials:

Selecting locally produced and natural building materials is consistent with off-grid construction's commitment to sustainability. Reclaimed wood, adobe, cob, straw bales, and other materials reduce the environmental effect of extraction and shipping. Utilizing plentiful resources in the surrounding area increases resource efficiency and lowers overall carbon emissions.

Using Rainwater Harvesting in Building:

It is possible to use off-grid ideas throughout the building process. Rainwater harvesting systems may gather water for construction, such as supplying water to workers on the job site or mixing concrete. By using this method, there is less need to use outside water sources during construction.

Managing Waste: Strategies

Waste management techniques are included in off-grid construction to reduce the environmental effect of building operations. This includes appropriately disposing of non-recyclable garbage, recycling building debris, and composting organic elements. The aim is to design buildings with the least possible ecological impact during construction.

Planetships:

With its use of recyclable materials, rainwater collecting, and passive solar architecture, earthships are a noteworthy breakthrough in off-grid buildings. These self-sufficient homes integrate environmental integration, energy efficiency, and sustainability into their off-grid architecture.

Living walls and green roofs:

Living walls and green roofs are examples of technology that improve a building's environmental performance. Green roofs include:

- We are adding more green areas.

- They are lowering stormwater runoff.

- We are providing insulation.

- Growing flora on the roof's surface.

Vertical gardens, often known as living walls, support biodiversity while improving interior air quality and aesthetic appeal.

Modular & Prefab Building:

Modular and prefab building techniques provide effective and adaptable off-grid options. Construction time and waste are decreased using prefabricated components made off-site and installed on-site. Buildings with modular components may be expanded and adjustable, making them suitable for a range of off-grid living situations.

Intelligent Home Technology:

Smart home technology can maximize energy efficiency and improve comfort in off-grid buildings. To improve overall energy efficiency and sustainability, homeowners may monitor and manage their energy use with the help of energy-efficient appliances, smart thermostats, and home automation systems.

Novelties in Eco-Friendly Materials:

The off-grid building is progressing because of ongoing advancements in sustainable materials. This covers creating materials with enhanced insulating qualities, a high percentage of recycled content, and little environmental effect. Sustainable material innovations seek to improve building practices regarding environmental impact and performance.

1. Obstacles and Things to Think About:

Zoning and regulatory challenges:

Zoning and regulatory issues might arise from off-grid living, especially if certain sustainable technologies are used. Zoning laws and local regulations may restrict unconventional building techniques or the installation of renewable energy sources. Getting involved with local government and pushing for supporting legislation are common steps toward overcoming these obstacles.

Requirements for Knowledge and Skills:

Adequate expertise and understanding are necessary to integrate sustainable technology into off-grid life effectively. Off-grid living requires knowledge of sustainable building methods, water filtration systems, and renewable energy system maintenance. Ongoing education and training are essential to guarantee these technologies' efficient and secure use.

Initial Expenses and Funding:

Although sustainable solutions provide long-term advantages, some people or groups may find the initial expenses prohibitive. It could be necessary to look into other funding sources or contact financial institutions that are aware of the long-term benefits to the economy and environment to get finance that values sustainable aspects.

Maintenance and system observation:

Sustainable technologies need constant upkeep and supervision. Examples include renewable energy systems, water purification systems, and off-grid building components. To guarantee lifespan and optimum performance, regular maintenance is required. To optimize efficiency, off-grid residents must take a proactive approach to monitoring and maintaining their sustainable systems.

Ability to Adjust to Local Climates:

Local temperatures and circumstances impact how well sustainable technology works for off-grid living. For best results, buildings and systems must be designed to adapt to particular environmental conditions. Considering flexibility is essential to the success of off-grid living, from identifying viable renewable energy sources to selecting construction materials fit for the local environment.

Finally, sustainable technology is a key component of off-grid life that embodies the values of self-sufficiency, environmental responsibility, and resilience. Off-grid people and communities embrace creative solutions for a comprehensive and sustainable living, from using renewable energy sources to implementing water conservation measures and sustainable building techniques. Beyond protecting the environment, there are financial savings, energy independence, and a smaller ecological imprint, to name a few advantages. Despite obstacles with legislative frameworks, expertise requirements, and upfront expenses, off-grid living's dedication to sustainable technology reflects a larger trend toward peaceful cohabitation with the environment. The sustainability and durability of off-grid life will continue to depend on integrating sustainable technology, promoting a more resilient and sustainable future as awareness of these issues rises.

Chapter 6: Homestead Skills and DIY Projects

6.1 Basic Carpentry and Construction

Proficiency in fundamental carpentry and building skills is an essential prerequisite for homesteading. This part explores the significance of these abilities, the fundamentals of carpentry, and how they are used to build homes that support the idea of sustainable and self-sufficient living.

❖ **The Importance of Fundamental Carpentry:**

Essential Homesteading Skill:

Beyond just being useful, basic carpentry is a fundamental homestead skill that enables people to build, fix, and improve their living environments. In the homesteading setting, when self-reliance is critical, the capacity to work with wood and build basic buildings becomes an instrument for turning concepts into actual, useful things.

Constructing and maintaining structures

Homesteaders often find themselves in circumstances where they must routinely construct or maintain buildings. Basic carpentry skills are essential for any project, whether creating furniture for the homestead, fixing a fence, or building a new chicken coop. A key component of homesteading is the ability to take unfinished materials and turn them into useful, long-lasting constructions.

Personalization and Flexibility:

Homesteaders can design their living areas to suit their requirements and tastes when they possess basic carpentry abilities. Homesteaders may customize their surroundings in impossible ways with mass-produced, prefabricated choices because carpentry's versatility ranges from creating inventive storage solutions to constructing shelters that fit the local climate.

❖ **Fundamental Carpentry Principles:**

Identifying the Features of Wood:

A profound comprehension of the properties of wood is essential to a basic carpentry concept. Various wood species have unique qualities, drawbacks, and strengths. By being aware of these differences, carpenters may choose the best wood for a given purpose, guaranteeing the robustness and lifetime of built products.

Accuracy and Measuring:

Measurement precision and accuracy are essential components of carpentry. The proverb "measure twice, cut once" emphasizes the need for careful preparation and exact execution. Precise dimensions are essential for carpentry projects to be structurally sound and professionally finished.

Joinery Methods:

The range of joinery methods that determine how wood is joined together is called carpentry. Dovetail joints, lap joints, mortise, and tenon joints are common joinery techniques. The intended purpose of the building, personal taste, and the necessary strength all influence the joinery method selection.

Tool Expertise:

One of the fundamentals of carpentry is tool proficiency. Carpenters use a wide range of equipment, from power instruments like drills and routers to hand tools like saws, chisels, and planes, to effectively complete various jobs. Mastering these instruments' appropriate use and upkeep is essential to attaining superior artistry.

Security Procedures:

A strong emphasis on following safety procedures is placed on carpentry. Adhering to safety measures is important while handling sharp instruments and heavy materials to avoid mishaps and injury. This includes using personal protection equipment (PPE), using tools properly, and being aware of possible risks at work.

❖ Utilization in Ecological Building:

Constructing Off-Grid Buildings:

An understanding of basic carpentry is essential for building off-grid buildings. Homesteaders use their carpentry skills to build houses that adhere to sustainable living principles, from constructing walls to roofing. When a building's resistance to weather is critical in off-grid living, the ability to design sturdy, weather-resistant structures is essential.

Making Use of Sustainable Materials

When building sustainably, carpentry often uses locally produced and environmentally friendly materials. Reclaimed wood is an option for homesteaders since it repurposes existing resources and lessens the need for new wood. The selection of non-toxic sealants and coatings also complies with the guidelines for designing healthy living areas.

Put Passive Solar Design Into Practice:

Using passive solar architecture in off-grid buildings requires some basic carpentry knowledge. This entails planning overhangs, putting in thermal mass components, and arranging windows strategically to optimize winter solar heat gain and reduce summer solar heat gain. Carpentry knowledge is necessary to build buildings that maximize natural sunlight for lighting and heating.

Building Eco-Friendly Fixtures and Furniture:

Carpentry goes beyond building components to include making environmentally friendly fixtures and furnishings. Using sustainably obtained wood, homesteaders with carpentry skills may create tables, chairs, cabinets, and other objects with less environmental effect than mass-produced furniture.

❖ Do-It-Yourself Self-Sufficiency Projects:

Building Infrastructure for a Homestead:

Homesteaders may build necessary infrastructure on their lands with the help of basic carpentry. This includes compost bins, making raised beds for farming, and erecting a fence to keep animals away from crops. These do-it-yourself initiatives improve the homestead's general operation and encourage waste management and food production self-sufficiency.

Fixing and Modernizing Homestead Parts:

Homesteaders often find that their current constructions need to be upgraded or repaired. Basic carpentry abilities allow people to solve problems quickly and independently, whether improving a storage shed, mending a broken roof, or strengthening a gate. One of the main principles of the homesteading lifestyle is independence.

Crafting Instruments & Tools:

The ability to carve extends to making the tools and equipment required for different homesteading jobs. Homesteaders may customize their tools to meet individual demands, creating durable garden tools and unique storage options for equipment, which increase productivity in everyday duties.

Constructing enclosures and shelters for animals:

Carpenters who homestead with livestock benefit from these abilities while constructing enclosures and animal shelters. The ability to plan and build animal-friendly facilities, such as a goat shelter, chicken coop, or beekeeping hive stand, improves the well-being of the people living on the farm.

❖ **Obstacles and Things to Think About:**

Restricted Material Access:

There may not always be easy access to specialty carpentry supplies in isolated homesteading areas. For their carpentry projects, homesteaders may need to be inventive and use materials that are readily accessible locally or repurpose existing buildings. This capacity to adapt is crucial for overcoming obstacles related to the availability of materials.

Education and the Development of Skill:

A commitment to continuous study and skill improvement is necessary to build and hone carpentry abilities. There can be a learning curve for homesteaders, particularly if carpentry is their first skill. Using instructional materials, attending seminars, and getting hands-on experience are crucial for developing competence and confidence.

The Effects of Wood Consumption on the Environment:

Carpentry presents questions regarding the effects of resource usage on the environment, especially when wood is used. The environmental impact of carpentry projects may be reduced by using recycled or reused wood, reforestation initiatives, and responsible wood procurement.

Security in Outlying Areas:

Homesteaders who operate in isolated areas might face particular safety difficulties. The isolation of homesteading and the distance from emergency services highlight how crucial it is to prioritize safety procedures. Proper first aid training and readiness for any mishap are essential for carpenters in remote areas.

Economic Aspects to Consider

While a basic understanding of carpentry helps one become self-sufficient, one must also consider costs. While some homesteaders may employ specialists for certain jobs, others may discover that DIY initiatives are more cost-effective. Careful thought must be given to balance the cost-effectiveness of do-it-yourself carpentry and the desire for independence.

To sum up, having a basic understanding of carpentry and building is essential to the homesteading lifestyle because it gives you the capacity to create, maintain, and modify your living areas in a way that adheres to sustainability and self-sufficiency. A spirit of independence and ingenuity is embodied by homesteaders with carpentry abilities who build off-grid buildings and make furniture and tools. Using these abilities is more than just a useful application; it's a way to maintain a relationship with the land, show a dedication to resource conservation, and embody the spirit of homesteading.

Learning carpentry fundamentals is still a life-changing experience for those looking for a practical, sustainable way to live off the land despite obstacles relating to skill development, material availability, and environmental concerns. Homesteaders add to the creation of their living areas and the larger story of self-sufficient and sustainable communities as they hone their carpentry skills.

6.2 Gardening and Food Preservation

The homesteading lifestyle revolves around gardening and food preservation, which stand for a mutually beneficial relationship with the land and a dedication to self-sufficiency. This section delves into the interwoven food preservation and gardening methods, highlighting their importance, guiding principles, and function in building a resilient and sustainable farm.

❖ **Gardening's Significance:**

Essentials of Homesteading:

Homesteading is based on gardening, which embodies the philosophy of growing one's food on the land. Homesteaders grow because it's a deeply ingrained tradition anchored in the cycles of nature and a way to produce wholesome, fresh food. The homesteader and the food they eat are directly connected via planting, caring for, and harvesting.

Increasing the Variety of Food Sources:

Through gardening, homesteaders may increase the diversity of their food supplies, lessen their need for outside markets, and encourage a diet richer in nutrients and variety. Homesteaders increase the resiliency of their food supply by growing various fruits, vegetables, herbs, and even medicinal plants. Because many plants have distinct nutritional advantages, this variety promotes a holistic approach to health and well-being.

Seasonality Flexibility:

Homesteaders use gardening's flexibility to adjust to changing seasons. Year-round agriculture is made possible by companion planting, crop rotation, and selecting types appropriate for the local climate. Homesteaders maximize growth conditions and minimize the need for outside inputs like pesticides and artificial fertilizers by cooperating with seasonal trends.

1. **Sustainable Gardening Principles:**

Regenerative and organic practices:

Organic and regenerative gardening methods are given priority, and synthetic chemicals are avoided in favor of natural substitutes. Compared to traditional agriculture practices, this strategy reduces environmental effects while preserving soil health and promoting biodiversity. Regenerative gardening requires companion planting, cover crops, and composting.

Conserving Water:

Water conservation is important to sustainable gardening, particularly in places with limited water supplies. Drip irrigation, mulching, and rainwater collection are a few strategies that assist in maximizing water consumption and guarantee that plants get enough moisture with the least amount of waste. The homestead's overall resistance to shifting climatic trends is enhanced by sustainable water management.

Planting companion plants and polycultures:

Companion planting and polyculture are encouraged in sustainable gardening as alternatives to monoculture. This entails growing a wide variety of plant types that are mutually beneficial and complementary. For example, companion planting deliberately places plants with mutually beneficial associations, such as improving nutrient absorption or discouraging pests. These methods lessen the chance of disease and pest outbreaks and enhance ecosystem resilience.

Heirloom and Seed Saving Varieties:

Seed preservation is a technique used in sustainable gardening to conserve and spread traditional types. A cultural and genetic legacy, heirloom seeds are often climate- and region-specific. Homesteaders support a link to the past of food agriculture and biodiversity preservation by gathering and distributing seeds.

Design of Permaculture:

Sustainable gardening is guided by permaculture principles, which emphasize the development of systems that emulate natural ecosystems. This involves planning garden designs that enhance productivity, reduce waste, and establish self-sufficient cycles. Permaculture design considers plant interactions, water movement, and sunshine to produce aesthetically pleasing and fruitful garden areas.

❖ **Use in the Preservation of Food:**

Methods for Canning and Preserving:

A prosperous gardener's natural next step is food preservation, which enables homesteaders to keep the bounty of harvest seasons for year-round sustenance. Farmers may increase the shelf life of fruits, vegetables, and other goods using canning and preservation methods, including fermentation, pressure, and water bath canning. Using these techniques, food waste may be minimized, and a consistent source of locally farmed food can be secured beyond the producing season.

Desiccating and Tackling:

Traditional food preservation techniques include drying and dehydrating, which include taking the moisture out of fruits, vegetables, herbs, and even meats. Homesteaders may produce shelf-stable food items using electric or solar dehydrators or basic air-drying methods. Dried foods are adaptable components for cooking and eating and maintain their nutritional content.

Tissue Cellaring:

A low-tech yet efficient way to preserve certain crops, such as winter squashes, apples, and root vegetables, is via root cellaring. Produce keeps longer in a root cellar because of its chilly, damp atmosphere, replicating the natural world. On the farm, root cellars may be built as an easy and economical way to preserve food.

Expiration:

As a traditional food preservation method, fermentation increases food's nutritional content while extending its shelf life. Homesteaders may use helpful bacteria to turn fresh vegetables into sour, probiotic-rich treats like sauerkraut, kimchi, and fermented pickles. Foods that have undergone fermentation improve digestive health and give meals a distinctive taste.

Curing and Smoking: Typical techniques, including curing and smoking, may preserve meatsking. Homesteaders who raise animals may cure and smoke meats to make sausages, jerky, or bacon. These preservation techniques not only give the meat unique tastes but also stop the development of bacteria that cause spoiling, extending the amount of time that may be stored without refrigeration.

❖ **Do-It-Yourself Sustainable Gardening Projects:**

Constructing Raised Beds:

Raised beds are a great way to practice sustainable gardening because they provide greater control over soil composition, better drainage, and less competition from weeds. Raised beds may be made by homesteaders themselves using materials like natural stone, reclaimed pallets, or untreated wood. Building raised beds is an easy and useful approach to maximize garden space.

Building Biomass Systems:

Composting is a key component of sustainable gardening, which adds organic waste rich in nutrients to the soil. Examples of do-it-yourself compost systems are simple compost bins constructed from recyclable materials or more intricate vermicomposting installations that use worms to speed up decomposition. Homesteaders may customize composting systems to match the size of their farming endeavors.

Building Systems for Harvesting Rainwater:

Collecting rainwater may lessen their dependence on municipal water supply and save water resources. Homesteaders may construct rain barrels, gutters, and downspouts as part of do-it-yourself rainwater gathering systems. Utilizing collected rainwater for irrigation reduces the amount of water utilized and its environmental effect.

Constructing Supports and Trellises:

Supports and trellises are necessary for vertical planting and space optimization. DIY projects involving the construction of trellises from bamboo, wood, or scrap metal are available to homesteaders. Climbing plants like tomatoes, cucumbers, and beans may be supported by these structures, which promote healthy development and maximize output.

Building Greenhouses and Cold Frames:

Many homesteaders want to extend the growing season, and they may do this by building their own greenhouses or cold frames. Early- or late-season crops may be grown in a protected environment thanks to cold frames, often built from salvaged windows. Whether they are basic hoop houses or more complex constructions, greenhouses provide regulated conditions for year-round farming.

❖ **Obstacles and Things to Think About:**

Management of Diseases and Pests:

Using natural and organic approaches to manage pests and illnesses is part of sustainable farming. Homesteaders might struggle to recognize problems and take appropriate action without using artificial pesticides. Important components of managing pests and diseases include using companion planting, drawing in helpful insects, and preserving the general health of the garden.

Duration and Level of Work:

Even if it pays well, sustainable gardening may require much time and work. Homesteaders sometimes have to juggle other obligations with their agricultural endeavors. Lowering the total burden may be achieved by implementing effective gardening techniques like mulching and no-till approaches.

The Acquisition Curve for Conservation Methods:

A learning curve may be involved in mastering food preservation procedures, particularly for novices. Homesteaders may need to devote time to honing their abilities, from knowing the correct canning techniques to getting the perfect taste balance in fermented foods. Learning may be accelerated by using reliable materials and consulting with seasoned homesteaders.

Climate and Growth Zone Difficulties:

Homesteaders must modify their gardening techniques to fit their growth zone and environment. Short growth seasons, high temperatures, or poor soil conditions might be obstacles. Climate-related issues may be addressed using soil amendment, hardy plant selection, and season extension strategies.

Juggling Preservation Techniques:

Selecting the best preservation techniques necessitates considering storage capacity, available resources, and individual preferences. To maintain a varied and well-preserved food supply, homesteaders may need to balance several preservation methods. It takes time and experimentation to identify the best mix of techniques for the demands of the farm.

In summary, food preservation and gardening are essential components of the homesteading way of life, representing the values of sustainability, self-sufficiency, and a close relationship with the earth. In addition to producing fresh, wholesome food, sustainable gardening techniques built on organic and regenerative principles strengthen the domestic ecology. Food preservation allows homesteaders to reap the rewards of their efforts all year, adding to the advantages of farming. Homesteaders use preservation techniques, such as canning, drying, fermenting, and smoking, to reduce food waste and maximize harvest potential.

These methods are also expressed in their cuisine. Homesteaders are better equipped to maximize their producing areas, save resources, and improve overall food security via do-it-yourself sustainable gardening initiatives. Despite obstacles relating to pests, time intensity, and climatic concerns, the pursuit of sustainable gardening and food preservation demonstrates a commitment to a comprehensive and independent way of life. Homesteaders improve their family well-being and advance the larger movement toward resilient and sustainable food systems as they hone their skills, exchange information, and adjust to the particular circumstances of their land.

6.3 Sewing and Clothing Repairs

Sewing and garment repair are more than just useful skills on a farm; they symbolize dedication to sustainability in clothes management, inventiveness, and self-sufficiency. This section delves into the ideas, applications, and transformational functions of sewing and garment repairs in the context of homesteading. It also highlights the value of these skills in promoting a resilient and conscious lifestyle.

❖ **The Importance of Stitching:**

Clothing Self-Sufficiency:

For homesteaders looking to become clothing self-sufficient, sewing is a fundamental skill. The capacity to manufacture, repair, and reuse clothes is in line with sustainability principles in a culture often defined by rapid fashion and throwaway clothing. Sewing at home may help homesteaders become less dependent on outside resources for their clothing requirements, which promotes a more deliberate and conscientious attitude to dressing.

Innovation and Waste Mitigation:

Homesteaders may recycle old or worn-out clothing by sewing them into new, useful ones, which displays ingenuity. This method complies with waste reduction principles by keeping clothes out of landfills and lowering the environmental effects of the textile industry. Homesteaders contribute to a more sustainable and circular fashion cycle by repairing and altering clothes to increase their lifetime.

Personalization and Expression of Self:

Homesteaders may personalize their clothes with sewing, expressing their own design choices and guaranteeing a snug fit. Sewing enables people to express their creativity and create a wardrobe consistent with their ideals, whether by customizing clothing or adding distinctive accessories. This customized method is in contrast to many conventional apparel products that are mass-produced and standardized.

❖ **Sustainable Sewing Principles:**

Repurposing and Upcycling:

Upcycling and reusing materials to give worn clothing or textiles a new lease of life is a key component of sustainable sewing. Homesteaders can upcycle worn-out jeans into a quilt or use leftover fabric scraps to create a patchwork jacket, among other creative ways to use old items. This approach is consistent with the circular economy's tenets, which call for constant resource reuse and repurposing.

Organic and Sustainable Textiles:

Choosing eco-friendly and natural materials is essential to sewing sustainably. Homesteaders may use eco-friendly materials like Tencel, hemp, organic cotton, or linen instead of traditional textiles since they have fewer environmental effects. This philosophy encompasses using materials with low chemical treatments and biodegradability, encouraging a more ecologically conscious and health-conscious attitude to clothing.

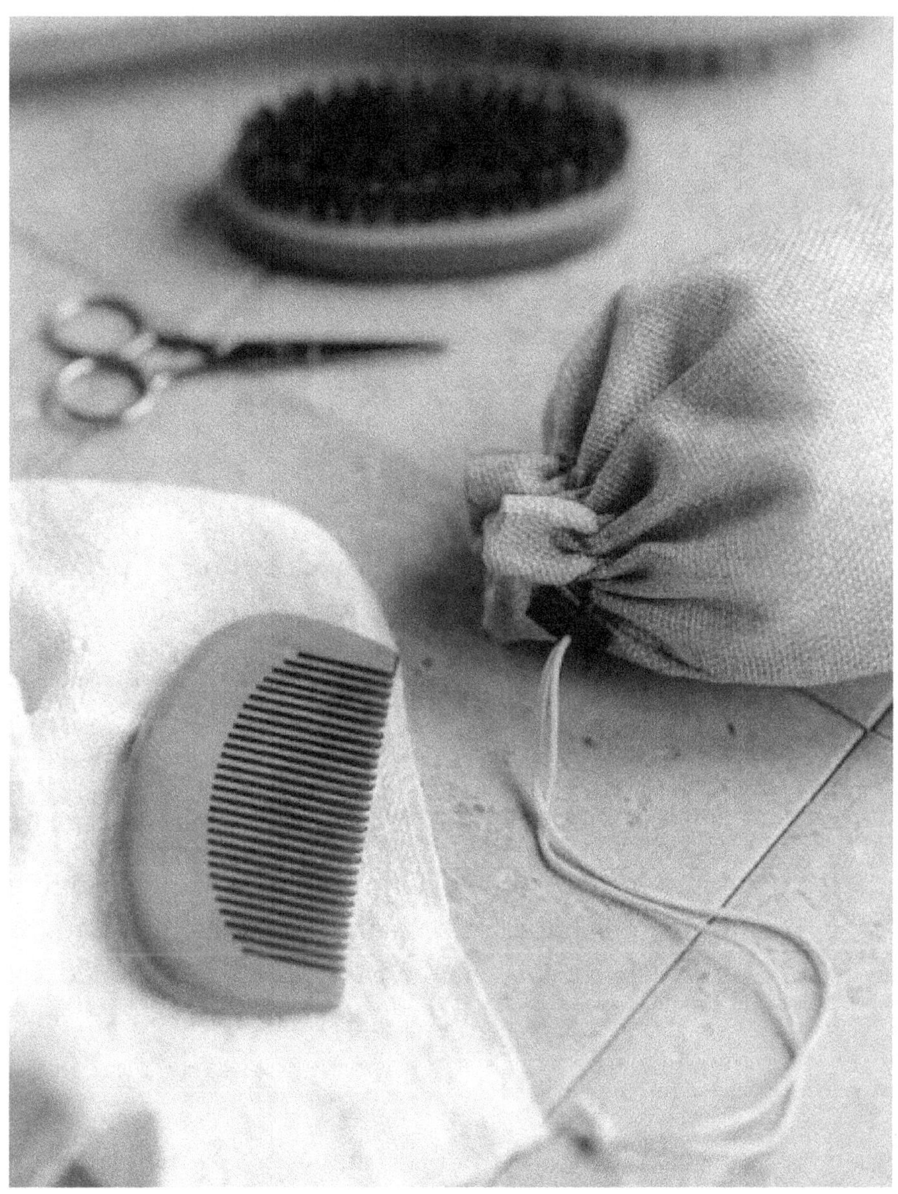

Techniques for Durable Construction:

Durable construction methods that guarantee durability and simplicity of repair are the focus of sustainable sewing. The resistance of clothing is increased by using high-quality thread, employing correct sewing techniques, and reinforcing seams. Sustainable sewing is a hobby among homesteaders who want to make clothes that last a long time and have less environmental impact by needing fewer replacements.

A Minimalist Approach to Clothing:

Sustainable sewing aligns with the minimalist wardrobe philosophy, emphasizing a well-chosen selection of classic and adaptable items. Homesteaders may reduce the total amount of clothing required by designing clothes that blend easily with an existing wardrobe. This encourages a thoughtful and less consumer-driven approach to fashion.

❖ **Utilization in Clothes Mendations:**

Repairing and Replacing:

Clothes repairs include a variety of tasks, but the two most important ones are patching and repairing. Homesteaders may patch worn-out sections, strengthen weak seams, and fix tiny rips. These treatments give textile items more character and individuality and extend their lifespan.

Changing Fasteners and Zippers:

Clothes repairs may be used to fix common problems like broken buttons, zippers, or other fasteners. Sewing-savvy homesteaders can fix damaged zippers, put buttons back on, or even update fastenings to improve the look and feel of clothing. This method reduces waste by keeping garments from being thrown out for little problems.

Modifying & Adjusting:

Sewing-trained homesteaders may adjust and customize clothes to fit well and accommodate evolving tastes. People may modify their clothes to fit their changing requirements and body types by cutting or reshaping seams and modifying hemlines. A more thoughtful and ecological approach to garment consumption is facilitated by tailoring.

Projects aimed at refashioning and transformation:

Clothes repairs are more than just cosmetic adjustments; they are also life-changing endeavors. Homesteaders may create a new look for their wardrobe without buying new materials by refashioning existing or thrifted clothing into new looks. Whether transforming a dress into a blouse or a shirt into a bag, these inventive projects demonstrate the adaptability of sewing on garment alterations.

❖ **Do-It-Yourself Sustainable Sewing Projects:**

Making Handmade Clothes:

Homesteaders may start doing do-it-yourself tasks to make their clothes. This involves making simple garments like T-shirts and skirts and more intricate ones like coats and outfits. People may pick materials, styles, and construction techniques for their DIY clothing projects consistent with their sustainable ideals.

Assembling a Stitch Kit:

Setting up a well-stocked sewing kit is a fundamental do-it-yourself activity for homesteaders. Essential sewing supplies, including needles, pins, scissors, and an assortment of threads, are included in a sewing kit. A stash of recycled and eco-friendly materials also helps homesteaders prepare for last-minute repairs, renovations, or artistic projects.

Making Recyclable Textile Products:

Making reusable textile objects to replace single-use ones is another aspect of sustainable sewing. Produce bags, linen napkins, and even environmentally friendly menstruation pads may be handmade by homesteaders. These do-it-yourself projects encourage a more environmentally friendly and waste-conscious lifestyle by lowering dependency on throwaway goods.

Developing and Designing Accessory Items:

In addition to apparel, homesteaders may design and make accessories like bags, hats, and scarves via do-it-yourself projects. The handcrafted quality of these accessories heightens the sense of personal connection to the goods while adding flair to ensembles. These items will last long because of the classic patterns and strong materials used.

❖ **Obstacles and Things to Think About:**

Learning Curve and Development of Skills:

Particularly for people new to the trade, sewing and clothes repair abilities may include a learning curve. It might take some time for homesteaders to learn and hone these abilities via practice, tutorials, and, if offered, community seminars. Developing new skills is continuous; people may progressively add more methods to their toolkits.

Accessibility of Ecological Materials:

Depending on the homestead's location, obtaining sustainable and environmentally friendly sewing supplies might be difficult. It can be necessary for homesteaders to look for regional and internet suppliers of notions, threads, and fabrics that complement their sustainable objectives. The broader dedication to sustainable sewing is bolstered by the support of morally and environmentally responsible suppliers.

Duration of Do-It-Yourself Projects:

Doing sewing tasks yourself, particularly when making clothes from scratch, takes a lot of time. Homesteaders must strike a balance between these tasks and their other duties. Effective time management and setting reasonable goals are crucial to guarantee that sewing is enjoyable without being too stressful.

Handling Intricate Repairs:

While many homesteaders can do simple repairs and modifications, more advanced repairs or changes require specialized knowledge. Consulting with knowledgeable sewers or other experts may be essential in these situations. Re-weaving cloth or resizing a garment are complex repairs that may require expert skills.

To sum up, sewing and garment repairs are integral to the homesteading lifestyle and represent the values of creativity, sustainability, and self-sufficiency. Upcycling, robust construction, and a minimalist wardrobe philosophy are the foundations of sustainable sewing techniques, which support a more deliberate and mindful relationship with clothes. The capacity to repair, modify, and make garments allow homesteaders to lessen their dependence on mass-produced apparel, lessen textile waste, and showcase their uniqueness via customized wardrobe selections.

These advantages are further enhanced by do-it-yourself sustainable sewing projects, which allow homesteaders to actively engage in producing their textile and apparel products. The goal of sustainable sewing aligns with the larger homesteading philosophy, which aims to create a life that is resourceful, conscientious, and closely tied to the concepts of sustainability, even in the face of obstacles relating to time commitment, skill development, and material availability. Homesteaders add to the resilience of their homesteads and the greater movement toward a more sustainable and conscious approach to fashion as they continue to exchange information, hone their sewing abilities, and embrace the creative possibilities within their wardrobes.

6.4 Soap Making and Natural Cleaning Products

Creating natural cleaning products and soap is a fundamental homesteading skill beyond utility. These projects represent the values of independence, care for the environment, and a dedication to a sustainable, chemical-free way of living. This section explores the importance, guiding principles, uses, and transformational qualities of natural cleaning product creation and soap production within the homesteading framework.

❖ **The Importance of Soap Production:**

Self-Sufficiency in Personal Care Items:

For homesteaders, manufacturing soap is essential to their self-sufficiency since it allows them to customize hygiene goods to meet their unique requirements. Hand soaps, body washes, and shampoo bars may all be created at home, giving users more control over the contents, avoiding potentially dangerous additions, and lowering their dependency on store-bought goods.

Natural and Chemical-Free Formulations:

Making soap at home makes it possible to create natural cleaning products without chemicals. Homesteaders make skin-friendly and eco-friendly washing products by using natural colorants, essential oils, and plant-based oils as components. This move away from store-bought soaps loaded with artificial ingredients is in line with a dedication to overall well-being.

Inventive Use of Ingredients:

Easily accessible materials are often used to produce soap, such as oils or fats from farm-raised animals or locally found botanicals. This creative use of ingredients supports a sustainable approach to producing hygiene products on the farm by promoting a circular economy.

❖ **Sustainable Soap Making Principles:**

Natural Substances and Vital Oils:

Natural components like shea butter, coconut oil, and olive oil are the priority when manufacturing sustainable soap. Essential oils are often used for extra skin benefits and scent. These ingredients have been selected concerning their environmental effect, and they are renewable and biodegradable.

Steer clear of dangerous additives:

Preservatives, harsh detergents, and artificial perfumes are common additions included in commercial soaps. By avoiding these dangerous ingredients, sustainable soap production produces skin-friendly soaps that lessen the amount of pollutants released into water systems.

Zero-Waste Methods:

Zero-waste methods may be embraced by homesteaders that embrace sustainable soap production. This entails reducing the amount of packing, making new bars out of leftover soap fragments, and utilizing reusable molds for soap forms. These methods support the larger objectives of sustainable living while also reducing trash.

❖ **Use in Organic Cleaning Supplies:**

Eco-Friendly Cleaning Products:

The principles of soap production may be used to develop non-toxic cleaning solutions and personal care. Instead of exposing themselves and the environment to the damaging effects of conventional cleaning chemicals, homesteaders may make their natural cleaning solutions for dishes, laundry, and surfaces.

Eco-Friendly Substances:

Natural cleaning solutions often include citrus peels, baking soda, vinegar, and other environmentally friendly chemicals. These materials provide cleansing without the negative effects of harsh chemicals on the environment. Using biodegradable and renewable materials is in line with sustainable practices.

Cutback on Single-Use Polymers:

Making natural cleaning solutions is a great way to reduce the single-use plastic bottles often used in professional cleaning supplies. To reduce packaging waste, homesteaders might use concentrate formulas and reusable containers.

❖ **Handmade Soap Making and Natural Cleaning Product Projects:**

Personalized Soap Bars:

One skill that homesteaders might practice is making their soap bars by hand. You may alter this do-it-yourself creation's smells, textures, and ingredients to fit your tastes. Making one-of-a-kind soap bars may be a fun and fulfilling project that gives everyday hygiene a customized touch.

Make Your Liquid Soaps:

Homesteaders could make homemade liquid soaps in addition to solid bars. You may use liquid soap for more than just hand cleaning; it can also be used as a body wash or shampoo. Making liquid soaps at home allows you to mix and match ingredients and try different smell combinations.

Natural Cleaners for Every Use:

Creating natural all-purpose cleansers for domestic surfaces is another do-it-yourself endeavor. Propane, water, and essential oils may create safe, chemical-free cleaning solutions. Homesteaders can customize recipes to meet certain cleaning requirements.

Eco-Friendly Cleaning Solution:

Homesteaders may sustainably approach laundry care by making their own environmentally friendly laundry detergents. Effective laundry detergents may be made at home using materials like borax, washing soda, and soap flakes without having the negative environmental effects of store-bought detergents.

Obstacles and Things to Think About

Managing Formulation Balance for Efficacy:

Achieving a balance between utilizing mild, environmentally friendly components and making sure the goods work as intended is necessary when making natural cleaning solutions and soaps. Homesteaders could need to test out several formulas before settling on one that cleans well and is sustainable.

Leaving Commercial Products Behind:

Switching from store-bought soaps and cleaning products to homemade alternatives could take some time. As they incorporate sustainable and natural solutions into their houses, homesteaders should be patient and willing to change their daily habits.

Shelf Life and Storage:

Compared to store-bought alternatives, homemade cleaning supplies and soaps—especially those formulated with natural ingredients—may need different shelf life and storage conditions. Maintaining the efficacy of these items requires knowing how to store them and keeping an eye out for when they expire.

Teaching Others About Eco-Friendly Options:

Homesteaders sometimes have to confront the difficulty of teaching relatives and guests about the advantages of eco-friendly soap and cleaning supplies. Fostering understanding may be aided by open communication and the exchange of knowledge on the benefits these alternatives have for the environment and human health.

To sum up, the production of soap and natural cleaning products are vital abilities for homesteaders to possess, as they symbolize the values of sustainability, self-reliance, and environmental awareness. Homesteaders may take charge of their hygiene and cleaning regimens with the help of these do-it-yourself projects, which align with their dedication to using natural substances, zero-waste methods, and a decreased dependency on commercial items. A comprehensive and conscious approach to homesteading is aided by pursuing sustainable soap production and natural cleaning products despite obstacles associated with formulation, switching from commercial goods, and teaching others. Homesteaders are essential in encouraging a more environmentally friendly and sustainable way of life since they research these methods, improve recipes, and impart their expertise.

6.5 Skill-building for Self-sufficiency

A key component of homesteading is developing self-sufficiency skills, which stand for a dedication to self-reliance, adaptability, and a close relationship with the land. In the context of homesteading, we examine the importance, guiding principles, practical applications, and transformational nature of developing skills for self-sufficiency in this section.

❖ **The Importance of Developing Skills for Self-Sufficiency:**

Empowerment via Information and Proficiency:

Building self-sufficiency skills equips homesteaders with the information and skills to independently care for their fundamental requirements. Gaining various skills increases self-reliance and decreases reliance on outside assistance in various situations, including food production, building, and maintenance.

Adaptability in the Face of Adversity:

Homesteaders deal with various difficulties, such as erratic weather patterns and uncertain economic times. Building skills helps people become more resilient by giving them the tools to adjust and solve problems. A homesteader's broad skill set is a toolbox for handling unanticipated situations.

Relationship with the Homestead Way of Life:

The homestead lifestyle, where producing one's food, constructing a shelter, and having the capacity to manufacture and repair things are all ingrained in everyday routines, is inherently skill-developing. A deep connection is formed between homesteaders and their surroundings via their affinity with the land and the practical aspect of learning new skills.

❖ **The Fundamentals of Developing Skills for Self-Sufficiency:**

Practical Instruction and Immersion Learning:

The concepts of developing skills for self-sufficiency place a strong emphasis on experiential learning and hands-on learning. Homesteaders participate in hands-on activities that enhance their comprehension and proficiency in various abilities instead of only depending on theoretical knowledge.

Regenerative and sustainable practices:

Building skills is in line with regenerative methods and environmental ideas. Homesteaders strive to learn skills that meet their immediate needs and support the long-term resilience and health of the homestead ecosystem, from organic agricultural practices to eco-friendly building methods.

Collaboration and Sharing in the Community:

While achieving self-sufficiency is a primary objective, developing skills often entails cooperation and community sharing. Homesteaders may build communal solidarity and collective resilience by exchanging information, expertise, and resources with neighbors and like-minded people.

❖ **Utilization in Diverse Homesteading Fields:**

Infrastructure and Construction of Homesteads:

Building up one's construction and infrastructure development skills is essential to starting and running a successful homestead. Homesteaders gain expertise in building methods that can resist harsh weather conditions by building irrigation systems, barns, and shelters.

Sustainable Agriculture and Permaculture:

Learning permaculture and sustainable agricultural techniques is essential to producing food on a farm. Homesteaders acquire the skills necessary to plan and manage a variety of robust ecosystems that support biodiversity and soil health while yielding a consistent crop.

The Management of Animals and Integrated Livestock:

A holistic approach to farming incorporates expertise in integrated livestock management and animal husbandry. Homesteaders foster symbiotic interactions between plants and animals by caring for the animals, controlling reproduction, and integrating livestock into the general ecology of the homestead.

Craftsmanship and Artisanal Proficiencies:

Homesteaders often acquire artisanal and handcrafting skills in pottery, blacksmithing, woodworking, and other traditional crafts. These abilities allow for the production of implements, cutlery, and ornamental objects, demonstrating a dedication to handicrafts and home-made goods.

Emergency Readiness and Basic Medical Care:

Building skills for self-sufficiency includes learning first aid and emergency preparation. To safeguard their and their community's safety, homesteaders pick up basic medical knowledge, practice emergency preparedness, and learn to deal with unforeseen circumstances.

❖ **Do It Yourself Skill-Building Projects:**

Construction and Maintenance of Infrastructure:

One practical method that homesteaders might use to learn construction skills is by doing tasks related to developing and maintaining infrastructure. Building raised beds for planting, fixing a fence, or building a new chicken coop are all tasks that improve the homestead's overall functioning.

Making Handmade Utensils & Tools:

Handcrafted tools and utensils, such as wooden spoons, hand-forged knives, or handmade baskets, are tasks that homesteaders may take on. Making these things improves artisanal abilities while producing useful tools that improve everyday living on the farm.

The Design and Application of Permaculture:

Homesteaders may independently develop and execute permaculture projects to produce regenerative and sustainable landscapes. This might include building composting facilities, installing water collecting systems, or planning and creating a permaculture garden.

The Care of Animals and Beekeeping:

Homesteaders can start do-it-yourself animal husbandry projects, including building hives for beekeeping, cattle shelters, or hen houses. These initiatives improve animal care and management while advancing the homestead's sustainability.

Workshops on Emergency Preparedness:

Putting on and participating in disaster preparation seminars is a group do-it-yourself initiative that improves the ability to deal with unanticipated situations. Topics, including community emergency preparedness, disaster response, and basic first aid, may be covered in these sessions.

Obstacles and Things to Think About

Time Invested in Acquiring Skills:

Building self-sufficiency skills takes a large time investment. Homesteaders may need to strike a balance between acquiring new skills and other obligations, keeping in mind that learning is a process that takes time to complete.

Adjusting to Differences in Geography and Climate:

The geographic and climatic variances that homesteaders experience affect whether skills are applicable. It takes thought and adaptability to develop skills appropriate for the homestead's unique circumstances, whether in a location prone to drought or extreme cold.

The initial outlay for resources and tools:

It's common for learning new talents to require an upfront investment in equipment, materials, and even instruction. Homesteaders should prioritize and budget for these expenses as they help them become long-term self-sufficient.

Ongoing Education and Maintaining Skills:

Building skills is a lifelong process that calls for constant maintenance and education. To continue being productive and resilient, homesteaders need to keep updated on developments in sustainable practices, adjust to shifting circumstances, and constantly improve their abilities.

To sum up, developing one's skills for self-sufficiency is essential to homesteading as it embodies the values of resilience, empowerment, and a connection to the land. Homesteaders embrace sustainability, participate in practical learning, and often work together with their neighbors. Gaining expertise in various fields, such as permaculture or building, shows a dedication to holistic living and a strong bond with the homestead way of life. The endeavor of skill-building adds to homesteads' continuous prosperity and sustainability, even in the face of obstacles about time commitment, adaptability to local circumstances, and the initial outlay of resources. Homesteaders are essential to promoting an independent and sustainable way of life because they work hard to hone their craft, impart information, and create a strong sense of community.

Chapter 7: Food Independence

7.1 Growing Your Own Food

Growing one's food is a fundamental aspect of the homesteading lifestyle, representing the values of sustainability, independence, and a close connection with the land. In this part, we explore the importance, guiding principles, techniques, obstacles, and revolutionary elements of homesteading when cultivating your food.

❖ **The Importance of Home Food Production:**

Independence and the Security of Food:

Producing food on your own fosters independence as it offers a reliable supply of nutrition unreliant on other influences. This approach improves food security by guaranteeing that homesteaders have a consistent supply of fresh, wholesome vegetables delivered right to their door.

Sustainability and Minimal Effect on the Environment:

Growing food in a home garden is a low-impact, locally-focused food production method consistent with sustainability ideals. Growing your food helps leave a lower ecological footprint by avoiding the need for long-distance transportation and dependence on industrial agriculture methods.

Relationship to Nature and Seasonal Cycles:

Growing your own food fosters a strong connection to the natural world and seasonal cycles. Homesteaders learn to listen to the cycles of planting, tending, and harvesting; they coordinate their operations with the seasons and develop a deep awareness of the biological processes involved.

Ensuring Quality and Nutritional Advantages:

Homesteaders can produce high-quality, nutrient-dense food because they have direct control over the gardening inputs and growing techniques. The nutritional value of homegrown food is higher than that of mass-produced alternatives since it is possible to raise a variety of crops and heritage kinds.

❖ **Grow Your Food Fundamentals:**

Sustainable and Organic Methods:

Organic and sustainable agricultural principles guide home gardening. Homesteaders steer clear of industrial pesticides and herbicides in favor of natural fertilizers, composting, and companion planting, which improves soil health and biodiversity.

Crop Variability and Associated Planting:

Cultivating various crops, fostering resilience, and lowering the chance of pest and disease outbreaks are all part of growing your food. Using plants that complement one another, or companion planting, improves the general health and yield of the garden.

Seasonal Planning and Planting Successions:

Homesteaders employ succession planting and seasonal planning to make the most of their limited land and increase their crops yearly. This calculated technique maximizes the homestead's resource use while guaranteeing a steady supply of fresh fruit.

Conserving Water and Optimizing Irrigation:

Growing your food requires a firm grasp of water conservation and effective irrigation techniques, particularly in areas with few water supplies. Methods including mulching, drip irrigation, and rainwater collection are used to save water and keep the soil wet.

❖ **Techniques for Vegetable Gardening:**

Raised Beds and Kitchen Gardens:

To access fresh fruits, vegetables, and herbs easily, homesteaders often create raised beds or kitchen gardens close to their dwellings. These more compact, closely tended areas allow for more productive gardening and are perfect for first-time growers or smaller locations.

Designing Permaculture for Food Forests:

Permaculture concepts influence the planning of homesteads' food-producing landscapes. Food forests combine trees, bushes, and ground cover plants to form a self-sustaining, diversified, and fruitful habitat. They are modeled after natural ecosystems.

Greenhouses and extending the season:

Homesteaders may utilize greenhouses to lengthen the growing season in areas with severe temperatures or short growing seasons. This makes producing food year-round and cultivating a greater variety of crops possible.

Shared Resources and Community Gardens:

Some homesteaders share resources and knowledge by taking part in communal gardens. Because raising one's food is a common objective, these shared areas provide chances for cooperation, information sharing, and a feeling of community.

❖ **Difficulties of Home Food Production:**

Environmental and Climatic Factors:

The temperature and other environmental elements that affect crop performance provide problems for homesteaders. Extreme weather, natural catastrophes, and unpredictable weather patterns may all be hazards to home garden sustainability.

Management of Diseases and Pests:

Managing illnesses and pests without artificial pesticides calls for close observation and action. Homesteaders may use companion planting, crop rotation, and natural predators to lessen the effects of pests and illnesses.

Duration and Level of Work:

It takes a lot of time and work to grow your food. Consistent labor is required for planting, weeding, watering, and harvesting, particularly during the busiest growth seasons. Time management is key to juggling these chores with other homesteading obligations.

Gardening Novices' Learning Curve:

Novice gardeners often experience a learning curve as they get acquainted with the unique requirements of various crops, soil management, and gardening practices. Persistence, constant learning, and flexibility are essential when developing gardening skills.

❖ **How Growing Your Food Can Change Your Life:**

Building Resilience and Patience:

Growing your food teaches you to be persistent and patient. Overcoming obstacles, adjusting to shifting circumstances, and patiently waiting for hard work to pay off foster a profound respect for the cyclical nature of food production.

Relationship to Natural Rhythms and the Seasons:

Growing their food allows homesteaders to engage deeply with the cycles of the seasons and the natural world. The springtime appearance of seedlings, the profusion of summer crops, and the winterization preparations highlight a homestead's cyclical existence.

Increased Recognition of Agriculture and Food:

Growing your food provides a hands-on learning experience that enhances your awareness of the complexities of agriculture. A deeper appreciation for the food on the table and a more conscious understanding of the larger agricultural scene are fostered by knowing the work and attention that goes into growing each crop.

Food sovereignty and empowerment:

Homesteaders who cultivate their food have a greater feeling of food sovereignty. Growing a sizable amount of food strengthens one's independence from industrial food systems and lessens the need for other nutrition resources.

To sum up, cultivating your food is an essential and life-changing part of homesteading, representing sustainability, self-sufficiency, and a healthy connection with the environment. Homesteaders overcome obstacles, adopt practices based on ecological principles, and feel a strong connection with the food they grow. Growing your food promotes resilience, patience, and a profound understanding of the interconnection of life on the farm, even in the face of pest control, climatic unpredictability, and gardening's time-consuming nature. A more resilient and self-sufficient future is largely shaped by homesteaders as they tend to their gardens, impart knowledge, and participate in the larger sustainable agriculture movement.

7.2 Canning and Preserving Techniques

Homesteaders need to know how to can and preserve food to prolong the shelf life of their crops and use the garden's abundance all year round. In the context of homesteading, this section examines the importance, guiding principles, techniques, difficulties, and transformational elements of canning and preserving.

❖ **The Importance of Preserving and Canning:**

Whole-year Availability of Homegrown Produce:

Homesteaders can enjoy the taste of their crops all year by canning and preserving. Regardless of seasonal availability, homesteaders guarantee a steady supply of wholesome, home-preserved items by harvesting fruits, vegetables, and herbs at their prime freshness.

Reducing Food Wastage:

By maximizing bountiful harvests, preservation methods reduce food loss for homesteaders. Make jams, pickles, and canned items out of excess produce that can be difficult to eat while fresh to cut waste and encourage a more sustainable way of eating.

Reduced Dependency and Self-Sufficiency:

Food canning and preservation help people become more self-sufficient by lowering their reliance on store-bought items. By keeping a well-stocked pantry full of their preserves, homesteaders may lessen their need for outside resources and live more sustainably and resiliently.

❖ **Fundamentals of Preserving and Canning:**

Safe and Sanitary Procedures:

Safety and sanitary measures are crucial when it comes to canning and preserving. Homesteaders follow set procedures to guarantee that the preserved foods are safe for long-term consumption and free of pollutants.

Harmonizing Textures and Flavors:

A careful balance of tastes and textures is necessary for successful canning and preservation. Homesteaders meticulously evaluate the flavor and texture of every product they preserve, modifying recipes to produce satisfying goods to use and hold up over time.

Appropriate Sterilization and Sealing:

For canning and preservation operations to be successful, appropriate sealing and sterilization must be achieved. Homesteaders use exacting methods to seal jars with a vacuum, keeping out air and microbes that can jeopardize the safety and quality of goods that have been preserved.

Recognizing pH Levels:

It's crucial to comprehend pH values while preserving fruits and vegetables. Certain foods, like tomatoes, must have their acidity levels carefully monitored to guarantee taste and safety. To ensure safe preservation, homesteaders often measure and modify pH levels.

❖ **Canning and Preserving Methodologies:**

Bath Canning in Water:

Water bath canning is a common technique for preserving high-acid foods, including fruits, jams, and pickles. Boiling water forms a vacuum seal in jars, successfully preserving the contents. Foods that naturally contain acidity as a preservation may use this strategy.

Condensation Canning:

Low-acid items, including soups, meats, and vegetables, are canned under pressure. Homesteaders may achieve greater temperatures and guarantee the eradication of dangerous germs such as Clostridium botulinum by using a pressure canner. This technique is essential for securely storing low-acid products.

Expiration:

Traditional preservation methods like fermentation improve tastes and nutritional value and extend shelf life. Homesteaders employ fermentation, using the natural process of helpful bacteria, to make products like pickles, kimchi, and sauerkraut.

Desiccating and Tackling:

Foods are dried and dehydrated to prevent the development of bacteria that cause spoiling. Homesteaders may preserve fruits, herbs, and vegetables in concentrated form by sun-drying, air-drying, or using electric dehydrators.

Chilling:

Freezing is a simple food preservation technique that keeps many foods' original flavors and textures. While fruits and cooked meals may be frozen for long-term preservation, homesteaders often blanch vegetables before freezing to retain color and texture.

❖ **Canning and Preserving Difficulties:**

Retention of Quality Over Time:

It might not be easy to keep preserved foods fresh over time. To maintain tastes, textures, and nutritional value for a longer time, homesteaders work hard to balance the preservation process.

Hazard of Pollution and Spoilage:

There is a chance that food can deteriorate and get contaminated, especially if the right procedures for sterilizing and sealing are not followed. Homesteaders need to be careful to follow the advice to stop dangerous germs from growing and jeopardizing the security of items that have been preserved.

Adjustment for Nutritional Preferences:

It might be difficult to modify preservation methods to satisfy various dietary requirements, such as those for vegan, gluten-free, or sugar-free foods. Homesteaders might investigate different preservation techniques and food selections to accommodate certain dietary requirements.

Storage Space Restraints:

The amount of preserved products may make storage space difficult. Homesteaders should schedule and provide:

- There is enough room for storing their canned and preserved goods.

- We are taking into account things like shelves.

- Temperature control.

- Cupboard space.

❖ **The Transformational Aspects of Preserving and Canning:**

Relationship to Tradition and Heritage:

Techniques for canning and preserving food often include a feeling of history and custom. Homesteaders have the opportunity to inherit techniques and recipes from earlier generations, which helps to preserve family culinary traditions and provide a link to the past.

Acquisition of Knowledge and Mastery of Skills:

Homesteaders may get extensive knowledge about food preservation and learn useful skills via the practice of canning and preserving. It encourages a lifelong path of study and skill development, from mastering taste combinations to comprehending the science underpinning safe canning.

Seasonal Sensitivity and Conscientious Eating:

Canning and preservation activities increase awareness of natural cycles and seasonal availability. Homesteaders learn to be more conscientious consumers, cherishing every season's bounty and storing their produce for later use when resources are few.

Decreased Dependency on Commercial Goods:

Homesteaders may lessen their need for commercially processed commodities by learning canning and preserving skills. This aligns with the ideas of self-sufficiency and a desire for more authority over the caliber and components of the food eaten.

In summary, canning and preservation methods are essential to the homesteading way of life because they represent the values of sustainability, self-sufficiency, and a link to culinary history. Homesteaders embrace various preservation techniques, including fermenting, drying, freezing, pressure canning, and water bath canning, while navigating issues with spoiling risks, quality retention, and space limitations.

Beyond only extending shelf life, canning and preserving fosters a strong connection with the seasons, a dedication to thoughtful consumption, and learning priceless skills handed down through the generations. Homesteaders are essential to preserving culinary traditions and developing a more resilient and self-sufficient future because they exchange recipes, hone preservation skills, and contribute to the larger conversation on sustainable food practices.

7.3 Raising Chickens for Eggs and Meat

A key component of homesteading is raising chickens for meat and eggs. They are a natural way to manage pests, fertilize plants, and provide a sustainable supply of protein. This section delves into the importance, tenets, practices, obstacles, and revolutionary elements of hen husbandry in the homesteading setting.

❖ **The Importance of Chicken Farming:**

Source of Sustainable Protein:

Producing eggs and meat from hens is a sustainable and renewable source of protein. Because they effectively transform feed into protein, chickens are an invaluable resource for homesteaders looking to become less dependent on outside food sources and increase their self-sufficiency.

Natural Fertilizer for Soil and Pest Control:

Chickens forage for insects, weeds, and larvae, which helps with natural pest management. Their digging provides healthy garden beds by aerating the soil, and their excrement is a nutrient-rich fertilizer. The homestead ecology is generally healthier as a result of this symbiotic interaction.

Possibilities for Education:

Homesteaders and their families have educational possibilities when they raise hens. Taking care of hens may teach kids about responsibility, life cycles, and animal husbandry. The practical experience helps to establish a link with the food-producing process.

❖ **Fundamentals of Chicken Farming:**

Kind and Moral Intervention:

Homesteaders raise hens on the tenets of humane and moral treatment. Ensuring enough feed, giving them access to a cozy coop, and giving them enough room for foraging are all ethical measures that improve the welfare of the animals.

Integrated Management of Livestock:

A key component of integrated livestock management is the mutually beneficial interaction that hens have with other components of the household. A comprehensive and integrated approach to homesteading may benefit from using chickens in companion planting, fertilizing gardens, and controlling pests.

Sustainable Methods of Feeding:

Homesteaders give sustainable feeding methods top priority for their hens. This might include using commercial feed, leftover food from the kitchen, foraged insects, and, in some situations, using permaculture ideas to create a closed-loop system in which chicken excrement improves soil fertility.

Frequent observation and medical attention:

Consistent observation and medical attention are fundamental components of ethical hen-rearing. To maintain the well-being of their flock, homesteaders keep a close eye on the general health of the hens, respond quickly to any disease symptoms, and provide any required shots or treatments.

❖ **Techniques for Growing Hens:**

Selecting Breeds of Chickens:

Homesteaders choose chicken breeds according to their objectives, such as focusing on meat quality, dual-purpose traits, or egg production. Rhode Island Reds and Leghorns are popular egg varieties, while heritage breeds like Sussex and Cornish Crosses are popular alternatives for producing meat.

Building Runs and Coops:

Building coops and runs are essential to giving hens a safe living place. Runs provide hens an area to go about and graze, while coops provide a secure place for roosting and egg-laying. Chicks are also shielded from predators and bad weather by well-designed shelters.

Nutrition and Feeding:

For hens to be healthy and productive, they need to be fed a balanced and nutrient-rich diet. In addition to conventional chicken feed, homesteaders provide access to pasture, grains, and leftover kitchen waste. The hens' age, breed, and intended use determine their precise nutritional needs.

Gathering and Managing Eggs:

The methods used for collecting and handling affect the quality of eggs produced. To keep eggs fresh, clean, and from spoiling, homesteaders gather eggs regularly. A safe and satisfying egg-eating experience is facilitated by appropriate handling, storing, and cleaning procedures.

Humane Processing and Slaughter:

A crucial element for homesteaders who raise chickens for meat is humane killing and processing. This entails using techniques that respect ethical standards and prioritize the animals' welfare. Both considerate and efficient processing guarantees that premium meat is produced for human consumption.

❖ **Difficulties in Growing Chickens:**

Predator Control:

One of the constant challenges of rearing hens is dealing with predators. Several creatures, including foxes, raccoons, and birds of prey, may harm hens and their eggs. To safeguard their flock, homesteaders use techniques including building a secure coop, keeping guard animals, and keeping a close eye on them.

Preventing and managing diseases:

Maintaining the flock's health requires close attention to disease prevention and control. Common poultry illnesses, including parasites or respiratory infections, may affect chickens. To prevent and treat infections, homesteaders isolate new birds, follow veterinarian recommendations, and put biosecurity measures in place.

Stabilizing Flock Behavior:

Managing a diversified flock or adding additional hens might make balancing the flock's dynamics difficult. There may be problems with the pecking order, and homesteaders must watch and step in to have a peaceful and fruitful flock.

Weather Factors to Consider:

Heat waves, cold snaps, and storms are extreme weather that may affect hens. When bad weather strikes, homesteaders must take extra care to protect their flock. They should provide shade, shelter, and suitable bedding to lessen the impact of temperature swings.

❖ **The Changing Elements of Keeping Chickens:**

Relationship to the Cycle of Food Production:

One may develop a close relationship with the food production cycle by raising hens. Homesteaders observe all stages of life, including chick hatching, egg laying, and meat production. Having this direct experience deepens one's awareness of the origins of the food on the table and increases appreciation for it.

Development of Work Ethics and Responsibilities:

Raising hens develops a work ethic and a feeling of responsibility in households and individuals. Regular work is needed for daily tasks, including cleaning, feeding, and gathering eggs. Connecting to nature and forming responsibility is especially beneficial for children.

Sustainable Gardening and Soil Improvement:

Because of their innate tendencies, hens improve gardens and create sustainable soil. Chickens offer nutrient-rich droppings, aerate the soil, and kill pests as they browse and scratch. This enhances the homestead garden's general health and fertility.

Autonomy and Decreased Food Miles:

Keeping hens is a good way to practice self-sufficiency and less dependence on other food sources. Because they raise their meat and eggs, homesteaders lessen the carbon footprint of the industrial food system and transportation. This independence increases the homestead's resilience.

To sum up, keeping chickens for meat and eggs is an essential and revolutionary part of homesteading, providing natural pest management, sustainable protein, and learning opportunities. Homesteaders follow the guidelines of humane treatment and integrated livestock management while navigating disease prevention, flock dynamics, and predator control issues. Raising hens is a transforming experience beyond simple animal husbandry; it improves soil fertility, cultivates a strong connection with the food production cycle, instills accountability and work ethic, and advances the more general objectives of sustainability and self-sufficiency. A more resilient and self-sufficient future is shaped in large part by homesteaders as they exchange information, improve their methods for rearing chickens, and participate in the larger conversation about sustainable agriculture.

7.4 Hunting and Foraging

In homesteading, hunting and foraging are age-old activities ingrained in the human experience and provide a sustainable and independent method of obtaining food. The importance, tenets, practices, difficulties, and transformational elements of hunting and foraging in the context of homesteading are explored in this section.

❖ **The Importance of Foraging and Hunting:**

Relationship with Nature:

Foraging and hunting provide a close relationship with the natural environment. By engaging in these behaviors, homesteaders understand the seasons, the habits of the local species, and the ecosystems they inhabit. This connection fosters a profound understanding of how all living things are interrelated.

Increasing the Variety of Protein Sources:

Diversifying protein sources is made possible by the homesteading lifestyle's integration of hunting. Hunting gives access to wild animals, enhancing the homesteader's diet with a diversity of meats, even if growing a garden and keeping hens are important aspects of a self-sufficient lifestyle.

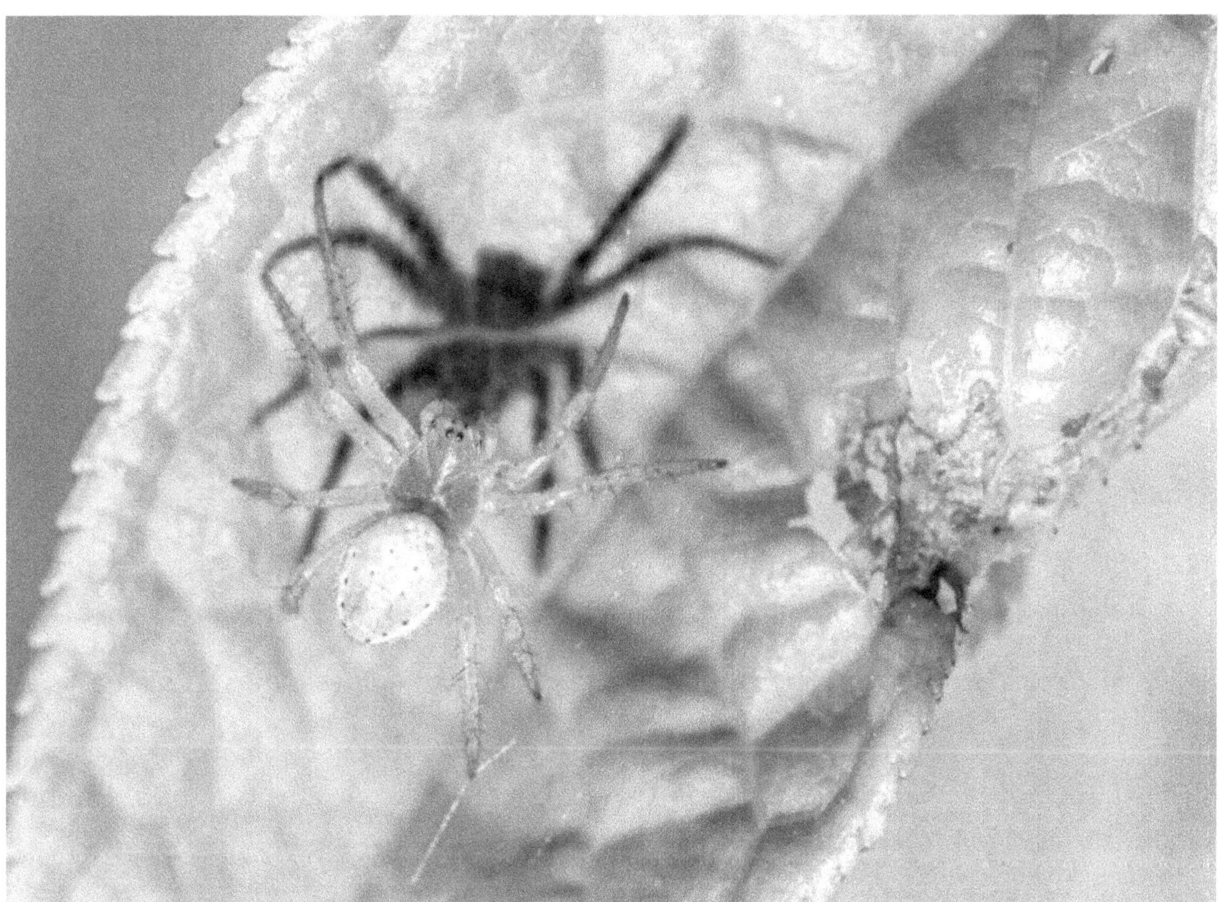

Tradition and the Development of Skill:

The abilities of hunting and foraging have been handed down through the ages, representing custom and cultural legacy. Acquiring these abilities helps homesteaders feel more connected to their roots and more independent since gathering food from the earth is a timeless and powerful skill.

❖ **Hunting and Foraging Fundamentals:**

Moral Gathering:

Ethical harvesting principles guide both hunting and foraging. Homesteaders place a high value on ethical and sustainable behavior, taking just what is necessary and making sure to have as little influence as possible on the surrounding ecology. Respecting animal populations and habitats is part of the ethical equation.

Understanding of the Local Fauna and Flora:

Thorough familiarity with the local flora and wildlife is necessary for successful hunting and foraging. Homesteaders get acquainted with the flora and fauna in their immediate environment, learning to recognize edible species, comprehend their life cycles, and spot possible threats. The basis for safe and efficient foraging and hunting is this understanding.

Stewardship and conservation:

Homesteaders hunting and gathering food often take up stewardship and conservation roles. They become champions for responsible land use, habitat preservation, and biodiversity conservation by actively engaging in the ecosystems they live in. This strategy guarantees that their actions have a beneficial impact on the environment.

❖ **Hunting and Foraging Methodologies:**

Pursing:

Identifying Species: Homesteaders acquire the skills to identify game species, comprehend their behaviors, and spot telltale signals of their presence.

Weapon Expertise: Being proficient with hunting implements, such as guns, bows, or other conventional weapons, is essential.

Ethical Harvesting: To reduce suffering and aid conservation efforts, ethical hunting entails precise shot placement and obedience to laws.

Processing and Preservation: To guarantee the quality and safety of the meat, one must be knowledgeable in field dressing, processing, and preserving game.

Grazing:

Plant Identification: Homesteaders research local plant species by identifying edible and non-edible plants.

Seasonal Awareness: Since foraging is seasonal, homesteaders must know when to collect certain plants at their prime.

Harvesting Methods: It's critical to comprehend how to responsibly gather wild plants without endangering populations or ecosystems.

Preservation Techniques: To increase the length of time that foraged foods are available all year round, they may be dried, canned, or preserved in various ways.

❖ **The Difficulties of Foraging and Hunting:**

External Elements:

Foragers and hunters face obstacles from weather, shifting animal populations, and altered environments. Unpredictable circumstances impact the success of these efforts. Thus, flexibility and knowledge of the natural dynamics of the area are necessary.

Respect for Regulations:

Regulations about sustainable practices and conservation apply to both hunting and foraging. Homesteaders must follow state and municipal regulations, get licenses, and respect limits and seasons. These rules must be followed for the preservation of species and the health of ecosystems.

Safety Issues:

While hunting and foraging, safety is of the utmost importance. To prevent mishaps, homesteaders must understand how to operate hunting equipment safely, identify possible environmental dangers, and take preventative measures. This involves being mindful of other people participating in outdoor activities and animals.

Mastery of Skills:

Gaining expertise in foraging and hunting takes time and commitment. Homesteaders must invest in their skill set, constantly honing their capacity to recognize different species, locate wildlife, and determine whether wild plants are edible. The continuous process of skill acquisition facilitates the success and longevity of these activities.

❖ **The Way That Hunting and Foraging Can Transform:**

Cultural Relationship:

Hunting and gathering food fosters a cultural bond with the land. Homesteaders uphold customs handed down through the ages, celebrating the abundance of nature and strengthening a feeling of cultural identity.

Independence and Adaptability:

Resilience and self-reliance are developed via hunting and foraging. Direct food procurement from the environment increases a homesteader's independence by lowering reliance on industrial food systems and building a stronger sense of adaptability to changing conditions.

Knowledge of Ecosystems:

Engaging in hunting and foraging activities enhances one's comprehension of ecosystems. Homesteaders learn to appreciate the subtleties of ecology, such as the interdependence of species, the precarious balance between predator and prey, and the effects of human activity on the environment.

Thank You for Using Sustainable Practices:

Homesteaders get a deep understanding of sustainable methods via the difficulties and pleasures of hunting and foraging. Their observations of the value of moral harvesting, conservation initiatives, and conscientious land use foster a dedication to maintaining the integrity and vigor of the ecosystems they live in.

To sum up, hunting and foraging are essential to the homesteading way of life because they provide:

- A close relationship with the natural world.

- A variety of protein sources.

- A deep cultural heritage.

Homesteaders follow moral harvesting, conservation, and stewardship guidelines while becoming skilled in species identification, weapon handling, and preservation methods. Environmental conditions, skill mastery, and regulatory compliance are challenges handled effortlessly and flexibly. The transforming qualities of hunting and foraging go well beyond only obtaining food; they include fostering a sense of cultural connectedness, developing self-reliance, learning about ecosystems, and developing a profound respect for sustainable activities. Homesteaders are essential to creating a resilient and environmentally aware future because they exchange information, hone their craft, and participate in larger discussions about sustainable living.

7.5 Developing a Sustainable Diet

A key component of homesteading is creating a sustainable diet, which includes decisions that put environmental responsibility, self-sufficiency, and health first. This section delves into the importance, guiding principles, techniques, obstacles, and game-changing elements of creating a sustainable diet as part of a homesteading lifestyle.

❖ **Why It's Important to Create a Sustainable Diet:**

Individual and Public Health:

Creating a sustainable diet is important for community and individual health. Homesteaders understand the close relationship between what they eat and their general health. They improve their and their community's health by growing and selecting nutrient-dense, locally-produced foods.

Diminished Ecological Effects:

Adopting a sustainable diet is consistent with environmental stewardship practices. By choosing locally produced and minimally processed foods, homesteaders want to lessen their environmental effects and the carbon footprint of food production, transportation, and packaging.

Boosting Regional Economy

Creating a sustainable diet requires a proactive approach to assisting regional farmers and producers. Homesteaders participate in community-supported agriculture (CSA) programs, visit farmers' markets, build direct connections with producers, and interact with their local food systems. This boosts regional economies and encourages a resilient feeling of community.

❖ **The Fundamentals of Formulating a Sustainable Diet:**

Seasonal and locally sourced foods:

A sustainable diet strongly emphasizes eating seasonal and locally obtained foods. Fruits, vegetables, and meats that are in season and produced locally are given priority by homesteaders. This method lowers the energy needed for long-distance transportation while assisting local farmers.

Whole foods and minimally processed foods:

Homesteaders base their diets mostly on whole, less processed foods. Examples of this are legumes, fresh veggies, whole grains, and unprocessed meats. They increase their intake of nutrients and reduce the environmental effects of industrial food processing by avoiding highly processed and refined meals.

Diversity and Sturdiness:

An essential component of a sustainable diet is diversity. Homesteaders work to create a robust and well-rounded food system by raising a broad range of crops and including different sources of protein. This strategy lessens the hazards brought on by crop failure or environmental condition changes.

Reducing waste and using compost:

Composting and waste minimization are integrated into the principles of sustainability. Homesteaders reduce food waste by organizing their meals, canning extra vegetables, and composting organic waste. Consequently, the compost that is produced improves the soil and establishes a closed-loop system in line with sustainable farming methods.

❖ **Approaches to Formulating a Sustainable Diet:**

Domestic Horticulture and Permaculture:

Permaculture and home gardening are essential to creating a sustainable diet. Homesteaders use permaculture principles to produce their fruits, vegetables, and herbs, resulting in resilient and regenerative food systems. This method produces nutrient-dense, fresh vegetables and strengthens ties to the land.

Animal Welfare and Local Production of Meat:

The homestead's practice of raising meat-producing animals adds to the diet's sustainability. Homesteaders place a high value on humane and locally sourced meat production. They often participate in free-range poultry farming, rotational grazing, and ethical animal husbandry. This promotes regional agriculture while guaranteeing a direct and moral supply of protein.

Food Preserving Methods:

Homesteaders use various food preservation methods to increase the quantity of seasonal crops available. Fruits, vegetables, and meats are often preserved by canning, fermenting, drying, and freezing. Thanks to these methods, homesteaders may benefit from a varied and nutrient-rich diet all year round.

Local markets and community-supported agriculture (CSA):

Developing a sustainable diet may be accomplished practically by interacting with CSAs and local markets. A common service for homesteaders is CSA subscriptions, which provide a consistent supply of fresh vegetables farmed nearby. They may also establish direct communication with producers by visiting farmers' markets, which promotes openness in the food supply chain and a feeling of community.

❖ **Difficulties in Creating a Sustainable Diet:**

Seasonal Restraints:

A difficult aspect of creating a sustainable diet is figuring out seasonal restrictions. Fresh food may not be readily available at certain periods of the year in certain regions.

To overcome this difficulty, homesteaders embrace seasonal diets, eat extra food, and look into other nutrient-rich options for the off-season.

Duration and Level of Work:

Cultivating a sustainable diet might take a lot of time and effort. Food preservation, raising animals, and home gardening require constant work and dedication. Homesteaders must discover effective and sustainable strategies to manage their food production while juggling these tasks with other obligations.

Both affordability and accessibility:

It might not be easy to get certain meals and to find sustainable ones at reasonable prices. Homesteaders in urban settings or places with little local agricultural production may find it difficult to get certain supplies. Creative solutions, like community gardening or the formation of local food cooperatives, are often necessary to overcome these obstacles.

Keeping Dietary Preferences in Check:

It might not be easy to balance dietary choices with environmental concerns. Homesteaders may adhere to certain dietary regimens, such as vegetarianism or veganism, which need meticulous preparation to guarantee a sufficient intake of nutrients. This entails investigating sources of plant-based protein varying crop types and considering ethical considerations when making dietary decisions.

❖ **A Sustainable Diet's Transformative Elements:**

Relationship with Food Sources:

Creating a sustainable diet encourages a close relationship with food sources. Homesteaders observe the whole food chain, from planting to harvesting or raising animals to producing meat. Making this link helps people appreciate the time, money, and effort that go into putting food on the table.

Wellbeing and Health:

Making a sustainable diet a priority leads to improved health and wellbeing. A meal rich in nutrients and low in chemicals and excessive processing should be the cornerstone of any healthy diet. As they shift to a more sustainable diet, homesteaders often feel more energized, vibrant, and well-being.

Community Adaptability:

Resilience within the community is enhanced by participating in local food systems and creating a sustainable diet. Homesteaders contribute to developing a strong and cohesive community through their active support of neighborhood farmers and producers. This resilience builds a network of support among families and individuals.

Effect on the Environment:

A sustainable diet is a key component of homesteaders' reduced environmental footprint. They choose foods that are in season, locally grown, and minimally processed, which helps eliminate packaging, cut carbon emissions, and make better use of natural resources. This awareness of the environment is consistent with larger initiatives to combat climate change and advance ecological health.

To sum up, creating a sustainable diet incorporating seasonal eating, local sourcing, and waste minimization is a fundamental part of the homesteading way of life. To create a varied and robust food system, homesteaders use home gardening, animal husbandry, and food preservation techniques — creative problem-solving and dedication address seasonality, time intensity, accessibility, and nutritional preferences. Creating a sustainable diet may lead to meaningful connections with food sources, better health, stronger communities, and less environmental impact. Homesteaders have a critical role in creating a more resilient, healthier, and ecologically conscientious future as they continue to improve their methods of producing and consuming food, exchange information, and participate in the larger conversation about sustainable living.

Chapter 8: Water Management and Conservation

8.1 Rainwater Harvesting Systems

Water management is essential to responsible homesteading in the quest for sustainable living. An essential part of this plan is rainwater collecting systems, which provide an environmentally responsible and proactive way to capture a valuable resource that is often wasted. This section explores the importance, guiding principles, techniques, obstacles, and revolutionary elements of rainwater collection systems in the context of homesteading.

❖ **Rainwater Harvesting Systems' Significance**

Preserving an Essential Resource:

Rainwater harvesting systems are important because they operate as a preventive step to solve the worldwide issue of water shortage. Homesteaders lessen their reliance on traditional water supplies, lessen the effects of drought, and preserve a critical resource by collecting and storing rainwater.

Sustainable Source of Water:

For homesteads, rainwater collection offers a decentralized, sustainable water source. Homesteaders collect rainwater for irrigation, animal watering, and domestic usage rather than depending on wells or city water supplies. Self-sufficiency and resilience are values that are in line with this sustainable strategy.

Reduced Stormwater Runoff:

Systems for collecting rainwater can reduce the amount of stormwater runoff. Heavy rainfall often results in runoff in traditional urban and suburban environments, which erodes soil and introduces contaminants into rivers. Reducing runoff by rainwater harvesting minimizes the water that enters the soil and hurts the ecosystem.

❖ **Rainwater Harvesting System Principles:**

Design of Catchment Area:

One of the main ideas of rainwater gathering is catchment area planning. Rainwater is collected at this surface, usually a building's roof. The design and composition of the catchment area affect the quality of the water gathered; metal or tile, for example, provide cleaner water than thatch or asphalt.

Transport and Filtration:

Rainwater is transported and filtered before being placed in the storage system—the gutters and downspouts direct water from the catchment area to the storage tank. Screens and mesh filters eliminate impurities and debris, guaranteeing that the water collected is pure.

Storage Volume:

Determining the proper amount of storage capacity is an important concept. It entails determining the homestead's water requirements and the area's average annual rainfall. Sufficient storage capacity permits extra water buildup for subsequent use and guarantees a steady supply during dry spells.

The first flush diversion

Rainwater collecting systems often include a first flush diversion feature to improve water quality. This keeps the first runoff from the storage tank, which can include contaminants from the catchment surface. The storage system receives the cleaner runoff that follows.

❖ **Rainwater Harvesting System Methodologies:**

Design of the Roof and Material Choice:

To efficiently capture rainwater, homesteaders give much thought to the layout and composition of their roofing. Smooth, steep roofs allow for more effective water drainage, and materials like concrete, tile, or metal are better since they last longer and have less of an effect on water quality.

Installation of Downspouts and Guttering:

The essential parts that direct rainfall from the catchment region to the storage system are gutters and downspouts. A smooth water flow is ensured by proper installation, which reduces the possibility of leaks and improves the collecting process.

Filtration Mechanisms:

Rainwater harvesting systems may include a variety of filtering methods. These include filters, screens, and mesh that clean the captured water of impurities and debris like leaves. Using efficient filtration ensures that the water in storage is of a high standard.

Positioning of Storage Tank:

Strategic considerations go into where the storage tank is placed. Elevated tanks provide gravity-based water distribution, which lowers the energy needed for pumping. Underground tanks provide space-saving options, which shield the gathered water from temperature changes.

Distribution and Pump Systems:

Pump systems may be used when gravity is not enough to distribute water. These pumps can transport collected rainfall to various homestead areas, assisting with domestic requirements, animal watering, and irrigation.

Rainwater Harvesting Systems' Challenges

Varying Amount of Rainfall:

The unpredictability of rainfall is a barrier for rainwater gathering systems. Water shortage may occur in areas with erratic or seasonal rainfall patterns. Thus, preparing for water storage and other water sources during dry times is important.

Original Setup Expenses:

Some homesteaders may find the early setup expenses of rainwater collection devices to be an obstacle. It might be necessary to make a sizable upfront cost to purchase high-quality components, appropriate installation, and enough storage. Many homesteaders, nevertheless, see this as a long-term investment in the sustainability of water resources.

Sustaining Conditions:

Rainwater harvesting devices need regular maintenance to operate at their best. Continuous activities include cleaning gutters, examining storage tanks for leaks, and testing filtration systems. System effectiveness and water quality might be jeopardized by neglecting maintenance.

Quality Issues:

The catchment region, roofing materials, and possible pollutants are some elements that affect the quality of captured rainwater. Concerns about water quality must be addressed by homesteaders, who must use suitable filtration and treatment techniques to guarantee that the gathered water satisfies safety requirements.

❖ **Rainwater Harvesting Systems' Transformative Aspects:**

Hydrological Autonomy:

Homesteaders who install rainwater collection devices gain water independence. Homesteaders build resilience against water scarcity or interruptions in municipal water supply by collecting and storing rainwater. This lessens their need for outside water sources.

Ecological Guardianship:

Resolving the use of rainwater collection is a sign of environmental care. Homesteaders actively promote the protection of natural water resources and sustainable water management by reducing stormwater runoff and dependence on groundwater.

Possibilities for Education:

Installing rainwater collection systems gives communities and homesteaders educational possibilities. Understanding these systems' guiding principles and procedures improves water literacy and raises awareness of the significance of water conservation on a larger scale.

Community Adaptability:

By establishing decentralized water sources, rainwater gathering enhances community resilience. Homesteaders using rainwater collection systems may pool their resources during crises or periods of water shortage, encouraging cooperation and assistance among neighbors.

In summary, rainwater collecting systems are essential to sustainable homesteading because they alleviate worries about water shortages and encourage wise water use. These systems are important because they help save water, provide a sustainable water source, and lessen stormwater runoff. Rainwater harvesting techniques guarantee effective and environmentally responsible water collection.

These techniques include catchment area design, conveyance and filtration, storage capacity, and first flush diversion. With careful planning and continuous dedication, challenges with rainfall unpredictability setup expenses at first, maintenance and water quality are overcome. Water independence, environmental stewardship, educational opportunity, and community resilience are transforming elements. A more water-conscious and sustainable future is largely shaped by homesteaders as they improve their rainwater-gathering techniques, impart information, and encourage wider adoption.

8.2 Efficient Irrigation Methods

To ensure that water is utilized wisely to support agricultural activities while avoiding waste, effective irrigation techniques are essential to homesteading's sustainable water management practices. This section delves into the importance, guiding concepts, techniques, obstacles, and transforming elements of effective irrigation techniques in homesteading.

❖ **The Importance of Effective Irrigation Techniques:**

Enhancing Water Utilization:

Effective irrigation techniques are important in their capacity to maximize water use, guaranteeing that water sprayed on gardens or crops serves its intended function without undue evaporation or runoff. Effective irrigation is crucial for maintaining agricultural practices while reducing environmental effects in areas with limited water supplies.

Preservation of Hydrologic Resources:

The use of effective irrigation techniques aids water resource conservation. Homesteaders actively contribute to the preservation of regional water ecosystems and the upkeep of the larger water cycle by minimizing water waste and runoff. This conservation method aligns with the ideas of environmental stewardship and sustainability.

Enhanced Harvest Outcomes:

Irrigation systems that are well-planned and operated increase agricultural yields. Plants that get enough water at the appropriate times are better able to absorb nutrients, develop more robustly, and resist environmental stresses. Higher crop yields may provide excess produce for the neighborhood and aid household food security.

❖ **Fundamentals of Effective Irrigation Techniques:**

Efficiency of Watering:

Watering efficiency is the top priority of efficient irrigation techniques, which seek to provide plants with the proper quantity of water without going overboard. This entails knowing how much water certain crops need, considering the soil's properties, and modifying irrigation techniques to meet the demands of particular plants.

When and How Often:

A key factor in efficiency is the time and frequency of watering. Reduced evaporation occurs when irrigation occurs at ideal periods, such as early morning or late evening. Furthermore, knowing the soil's ability to retain water helps determine how often to rinse to keep the soil wet without going overboard.

Design of Irrigation Systems:

A basic premise is to design irrigation systems to meet the demands of the homestead. This entails deciding on suitable irrigation techniques, including soaker hoses or drip irrigation, and setting up the system configuration to guarantee even water distribution across the growing area.

Observing and Modifying:

Sufficient irrigation requires ongoing observation and modification. Homesteaders should routinely check their soil's moisture content, monitor their plants' health, and modify their watering plans in response to the weather. This adaptable strategy guarantees efficient water consumption and prevents over- and underwatering.

❖ **Techniques for Effective Watering:**

Drip Watering:

Water loss from evaporation or runoff is reduced when plants get water straight from the root system using drip irrigation, a very effective technique. This technique offers exact control over water distribution and works particularly well for gardens, orchards, and row crops.

Hose Soaker:

Water gently seeps into the soil along the length of soaker hoses because they are porous. Soaker hoses provide a gentle and effective approach to water garden beds, flower borders, and vegetable rows when placed at the base of the plants. They reduce evaporation, lessen water splashing, and encourage deep root penetration.

Blending:

A non-irrigation method that improves water efficiency is mulching. When applied around plants, mulch helps maintain soil moisture, inhibits weed development, and lowers soil temperature. Mulching helps save water by lowering the demand for regular watering.

Integrating Rainwater Harvesting:

Efficiency is increased when irrigation systems are integrated with rainwater gathering. Rainwater harvesting lessens dependency on outside water sources by allowing it to be stored and used for irrigation during dry spells. The concepts of self-sufficiency and water sustainability are in line with this strategy.

❖ Difficulties with Effective Irrigation Techniques:

Original Setup Expenses:

The initial setup expenses are one of the issues with effective irrigation techniques. Purchasing soaker hoses, drip irrigation systems, or other water-saving devices might cost money upfront. Many homesteaders, however, see this investment as a long-term tactic that will pay off in the form of increased agricultural yields and water savings.

Upkeep of the System:

Frequent maintenance is necessary for effective irrigation systems to function at their best. Burst soaker hoses or clogged drip irrigation emitters may impact water distribution. Homesteaders must schedule regular system maintenance, including checking and replacing worn-out parts.

Knowledge Curve:

For homesteaders, using effective irrigation techniques may require a learning curve. It takes expertise and experience to adjust irrigation schedules, diagnose system problems, and comprehend the water requirements of various plants. The more homesteaders use these techniques, the more effectively they utilize water.

Variable Water Requirements for Crops:

It may be difficult to manage the changes in crops' water needs at various stages of development. While some plants prefer drier circumstances, others may need extra water while blooming or fruiting. Efficient irrigation techniques must consider these changes in crop water requirements.

❖ Revolutionary Features of Effective Irrigation Techniques:

Preservation of Resources:

Water for present and future generations is preserved via efficient irrigation techniques, which helps conserve resources. Homesteaders actively engage in sustainable water management strategies that complement larger environmental conservation initiatives by reducing water waste and maximizing consumption.

Enhanced Fortitude

Effective irrigation techniques increase a homestead's ability to withstand water shortages and climatic change. Homesteads are better prepared to weather dry spells and maintain agricultural output and food security when they use water wisely.

Financial Savings:

For homesteaders, efficient irrigation means financial savings. Homesteaders may save their operating expenses and water bills by using less water. Furthermore, the possibility of higher agricultural yields supports economic sustainability by supplying excess products for personal use or local markets.

Effect on the Environment:

Effective irrigation techniques have a favorable effect on the environmental impact of homesteading. Homesteaders lessen their influence on nearby water ecosystems, lessen soil erosion, and help create a more balanced water cycle in their immediate surroundings by using less runoff and water.

In summary, effective irrigation techniques are essential to homesteaders' responsible use of water resources as they maximize agricultural yields, save water, and build resource resilience. The concepts of irrigation system design, timing, watering efficiency, and continuous monitoring guide these techniques. Drip irrigation, soaker hoses, mulching, and rainwater collection may improve the homestead's water efficiency.

With a dedication to continuous development, obstacles about initial setup expenses, system upkeep, the learning curve, and changing crop water needs are overcome. The conservation of resources, heightened resilience, financial savings, and favorable environmental effects are among the transformational features of effective irrigation techniques. A more sustainable and water-conscious future is largely shaped by homesteaders as they exchange information, improve irrigation techniques, and encourage wider use.

8.3 Water Purification Techniques

In homesteading, water filtration methods are crucial because they provide a clean, dependable water supply for drinking, cooking, and gardening, among other uses. This section delves into the importance, guiding concepts, tactics, obstacles, and transforming elements of water purification methods in a homesteading setting.

The Importance of Methods for Water Purification

Providing Clean Drinking Water:

The capacity of water purification methods to provide safe drinking water is its main relevance. Homesteaders understand how crucial it is for their families to have access to clean water. Filtering water may help eliminate germs, pollutants, and other things that might harm your health if you drink it.

Safeguarding Agricultural Methods:

Water filtration is not only for drinking; it also protects farming operations. Plants develop more robustly by preventing the entrance of dangerous materials into the soil and crops by irrigation with purified water, and the risk of waterborne illnesses that affect both plants and animals is reduced.

Reducing the Effect on the Environment:

Purifying water can lessen the negative effects of farming on the environment. By treating water before releasing it into the environment, local ecosystems are preserved, natural water sources are kept clean, and the general health of aquatic habitats is supported.

❖ **Fundamentals of Water Purification Methods:**

Entire Contaminant Elimination:

Complete contamination removal is a prerequisite for effective water purification. This entails dealing with various contaminants, including chemicals, heavy metals, bacteria, viruses, parasites, and sediments. To protect the purity of their water supply, homesteaders prioritize filtration techniques that address a variety of possible contaminants.

Self-sufficiency and Sustainability:

When choosing water purifying methods, sustainability and self-sufficiency are taken into consideration. The goal of homesteading is to use sustainable practices that don't depend on outside resources and can be maintained over an extended period. This fits well with homesteading's larger philosophy of self-sufficiency.

Adjustment to Hydric Resources:

Techniques for purifying water must be flexible enough to work with various water sources. Depending on whether homesteaders use surface water, rainfall, or well water, the purifying techniques should be appropriate for the particular qualities and possible pollutants found in each source.

Integration with Systems for Water Storage:

Systems for storing water are often integrated with purification procedures. Keeping the stored water clean and safe for various applications entails cleaning the water before it reaches storage tanks. The water supply on the homestead is more resilient overall when integrated with storage systems.

❖ **Techniques for Water Purification Methodologies:**

Filtration Mechanisms:

One popular and efficient technique for purifying water is filtration. To physically remove particles, pollutants, and toxins from the water, homesteaders employ a variety of filters, including ceramic filters, sediment filters, and activated carbon filters. When treating water, filtration is often the first step.

Simmering and Heating:

A tried-and-true technique for ridding water of microbiological pollutants is to boil it. Another method is pasteurization, which is done at temperatures lower than boiling. These methods provide a simple way to guarantee the microbiological safety of water by killing or inactivating bacteria, viruses, and parasites.

Chemical Cleansing:

Chemical disinfection eliminates or neutralizes germs in water by adding chemicals such as chlorine dioxide, iodine, or chlorine. Homesteaders may chemically treat water to make it safe to drink by using pills, drops, or solutions. For disinfection to be successful, dose and contact duration must be considered.

Treatment using UV Light:

By using ultraviolet light to damage bacteria' DNA, UV therapy stops them from reproducing. UV purifiers work well against viruses, bacteria, and protozoa. This technique works well for purifying clear water sources and doesn't need chemicals or energy.

RO, or reverse osmosis:

A semipermeable membrane is used in the filtering process known as reverse osmosis to extract bigger particles, molecules, and ions from water. Salts, heavy metals, and viruses are just a few pollutants that RO systems are good at eliminating. They are often used to clean drinking water.

Distilleries:

In the distillation process, water is heated to produce steam, which is then condensed into liquid. Pathogens and heavy metals are among the pollutants left behind after this method eliminates impurities that do not evaporate. Although distillation is a dependable process for producing pure water, it may be energy-intensive.

Needs for Energy:

Certain methods of purifying water, such as distillation and reverse osmosis, could need a lot of energy. For homesteaders looking for sustainable and off-grid alternatives, this might be a problem. When selecting the best purification technique, the energy economy must be balanced with the demand for clean water.

Reconstruction and upkeep:

Regular maintenance and the periodic replacement of parts like UV lamps or filters are necessary for water purification systems. To ensure that purifying systems continue to work overtime, homesteaders must commit time and resources. Water quality may be compromised by maintenance neglect.

Cost-related factors:

Certain homesteaders find it difficult to afford the costs of implementing certain water purification methods, particularly those with limited resources. Reverse osmosis units, UV purifiers, and high-quality filtration systems may have initial expenditures that require cautious budgeting. Nonetheless, many homesteaders see these expenses as necessary investments in their families' health and welfare.

Adjusting to the Quality of Water:

The original quality of the water supply might affect how efficient certain purification methods are. A mixture of filtration techniques or further pretreatment may be necessary for water with significant concentrations of pollutants, heavy metals, or silt. For best outcomes, purification procedures must be tailored to the unique characteristics of the water.

❖ **Transformative Features of Methods for Water Purification:**

Wellbeing and Health:

Techniques for purifying water may significantly improve homesteaders' health and well-being. Waterborne illness risk is decreased when clean, safe water is available for drinking and other domestic uses, improving general health and guaranteeing a better standard of living.

Ecological Guardianship:

Using environmentally friendly water filtration methods aligns with the ideas of environmental responsibility. Homesteaders emphasizing environmentally friendly practices help preserve water supplies and keep nearby ecosystems uncontaminated.

Independence and Sturdiness:

Techniques for purifying water improve homesteads' resilience and self-sufficiency. Homesteaders who can purify water from many sources are less reliant on outside water sources and are better prepared to deal with unforeseen circumstances like droughts or interruptions in municipal water supply.

Possibilities for Education:

Putting water filtration methods into practice gives homesteaders and their communities educational opportunities. Understanding the fundamentals and practices of water treatment increases water literacy, promotes responsible water usage, and raises awareness of the significance of water quality.

In summary, water filtration methods are essential to the success of homesteading, as they guarantee the availability of clean drinking water, safeguard agricultural methods, and reduce environmental effects. The concepts of complete pollutant removal, sustainability, adaptability to water sources, and interaction with water storage systems guide the selection and use of purification techniques. Homesteaders use practical techniques, including distillation, boiling, chemical disinfection, reverse osmosis, filtration systems, and UV treatment to guarantee the cleanliness of their water.

Careful design and continuous dedication are used to handle issues with energy needs, maintenance, financial concerns, and adaptability to water quality. Improved health and well-being, environmental stewardship, self-sufficiency, resilience, and educational possibilities are some transformational features of water purification procedures. A more water-conscious and sustainable future is largely shaped by homesteaders as they improve their methods of purifying water, impart information, and encourage wider adoption.

Here's a text-based table summarizing the key points for the topic "Water Purification Techniques":

Aspect	Description
Significance	Ensuring safe drinking water, protecting agricultural practices, and mitigating environmental impact.

Principles	Comprehensive contaminant removal, sustainability, adaptation to water sources, and integration with water storage systems.
Methodologies	Filtration systems, boiling and pasteurization, chemical disinfection, ultraviolet treatment, reverse osmosis, and distillation.
Challenges	Energy requirements, maintenance and replacement, cost considerations, and adaptation to water quality.
Transformative Aspects	Improved health and well-being, environmental stewardship, self-sufficiency, resilience, and educational opportunities.
Conclusion	Water purification techniques are integral for homesteading, providing safe drinking water, protecting agriculture, and mitigating environmental impact. Principles include contaminant removal, sustainability, adaptation, and integration. Various methods address challenges, offering transformative benefits for health, sustainability, and community education.

This table summarizes the key aspects of water purification techniques, including their significance, guiding principles, methodologies, challenges, transformative aspects, and overall conclusion.

8.4 Conservation Practices

In homesteading, conservation techniques are essential to guaranteeing ethical and sustainable use of water resources. This section explores the importance, guiding concepts, techniques, obstacles, and transformational elements of putting conservation methods into practice on the farm.

❖ **Conservation Practices' Significance:**

Keeping Natural Resources Safe:

The conservation of natural resources, especially water, is greatly aided by conservation techniques. Homesteaders know the limited availability of water resources and that ecosystem sustainability, ecological balance, and water quality depend on appropriate usage.

Reducing the Effect on the Environment:

When conservation measures are implemented, the homestead's water consumption has a less negative environmental effect. Homesteaders safeguard the wider environment and local ecosystems by limiting water runoff, decreasing soil erosion, and avoiding contaminating water sources.

Encouragement of Sustainability

The overarching objective of homesteading sustainability is in line with conservation techniques. Homesteaders add to the long-term sustainability of their agricultural operations by minimizing water waste, improving irrigation, and using water-efficient practices, guaranteeing resource availability for future generations.

1. **Conservation Practices Fundamentals:**

Effective Use of Water:

One of the cornerstones of conservation strategies is the efficient use of water. Homesteaders aim to extract as much value as possible from every drop of water, whether it is utilized for cattle, domestic usage, or irrigation. This entails limiting water loss, scheduling irrigations optimally, and choosing water-efficient equipment.

Control of Erosion:

Controlling soil erosion is one aspect of conservation strategies that may affect water quality and cause sedimentation in bodies of water. On the farm, methods like mulching, cover crops, and contour plowing assist in stabilizing the soil, reducing erosion, and improving water quality.

Preventing Pollution:

One of the main tenets of conservation techniques is pollution prevention. Homesteaders use techniques to prevent pollutants from entering water sources, such as chemicals or agricultural runoff. Pollution may be avoided by disposing of garbage properly, using pesticides and fertilizers sensibly, and keeping vegetative buffers in place.

Protecting Water Sources:

A feeling of accountability for maintaining and managing water sources is a component of stewardship. Practices that guarantee the sustainability of aquifers, wells, and other water sources are given top priority by homesteaders. This can include consistent water quality testing, well upkeep, and adherence to sustainable withdrawal rates.

❖ **Conservation Practice Methodologies:**

Technologies for Water Efficiency and Drip Irrigation:

Techniques for maximizing water consumption in agriculture include drip irrigation systems and other water-efficient technology. By supplying water straight to the roots of plants, these systems reduce water loss from evaporation or runoff. Household gadgets that consume less water can help with conservation.

Rain Gardens with Permeable Surfaces:

Homesteaders use rain gardens and permeable surfaces to combat runoff and soil erosion. Instead of producing runoff, permeable pavements let rainfall seep into the soil. Strategically planned rain gardens can reduce erosion, filter pollutants, replenish groundwater, and collect and absorb rainfall.

Crop rotation and cover crops:

Crop rotation and cover crops are two agricultural techniques that improve soil health, reduce erosion, and help save water. Cover crops supply organic matter, enhance water retention, and prevent soil erosion. Crop rotation reduces the need for excessive watering by diversifying plant kinds and minimizing the depletion of certain nutrients.

Systems for Recycling Greywater:

To recycle greywater for irrigation, domestic wastewater must be collected and treated, except toilet water. By installing greywater recycling systems, you may promote sustainable water usage in gardening and landscaping while lowering the strain on freshwater supplies for irrigation.

Participation in Community and Education:

Beyond private homesteads, conservation efforts often include community outreach and education. Homesteaders participate in neighborhood campaigns, training sessions, and instructional activities supporting water conservation. Broader conservation initiatives benefit from information sharing and developing a feeling of communal responsibility.

❖ Difficulties with Conservation Methods:

Alterations in behavior

Making behavioral adjustments is one of the difficulties with conservation methods. Changing perspective and daily routines may be necessary to adopt water-efficient behaviors, such as taking shorter showers or modifying irrigation techniques. Teaching a conservation ethic and overcoming reluctance to change may take some time.

Initial Implementation Expenses:

The initial infrastructure expenses associated with implementing conservation methods, such as building permeable surfaces, drip irrigation systems, or greywater recycling systems, may be incurred. Even while these expenditures often result in long-term savings, some homesteaders may find the initial costs prohibitive, particularly those with limited resources.

Adjustment to Regional Circumstances:

It is necessary to tailor conservation techniques to the area's specifics, considering the climate, type of soil, and water availability. It could be necessary to adapt what functions effectively in one area to the unique possibilities and problems the local environment presents. This flexibility requires a sophisticated comprehension of the environment of the homestead.

Community Arrangement:

It might not be easy to coordinate conservation activities inside a community. Effective communication and community participation are necessary to align varied viewpoints, address varying degrees of awareness, and ensure consistent adoption of conservation policies across the community.

❖ **Conservation Practices' Transformative Aspects:**

Manage Water Resources Sustainably:

By promoting responsible use, replenishment, and availability of water resources for future demands, conservation methods help to ensure sustainable water management. The transforming element is the transition from resource extraction to stewardship, which fosters ecological balance and resilience.

Health of Ecosystems and Biodiversity:

The richness and health of nearby ecosystems are transformed when homesteaders use conservation techniques. A balanced and resilient ecology is fostered by homesteads, which become refuges for various plant and animal species via pollution reduction, erosion management, and the preservation of natural habitats.

A Cultural Turn Away From Pollution:

Adopting conservation measures starts a cultural movement that makes everyone in the community more ecologically and water-conscious. This change entails emphasizing sustainability in day-to-day operations, encouraging a feeling of responsibility for environmental care, and acknowledging the interconnectedness of human activity and the natural world.

Enhanced Capability to Handle Variability in Climate:

Conservation techniques improve the homestead's capacity to withstand fluctuations in the climate. Homesteads may better resist the difficulties by shifting weather patterns, such as droughts, floods, and other severe occurrences, by optimizing water management, reducing erosion, and fostering soil health.

To sum up, conservation techniques are essential to homesteading's sustainable management of water resources. The concepts of stewardship, erosion control, pollution avoidance, and effective water use guide these methods. Some methodologies used include water-efficient technology, porous surfaces, greywater recycling, and community involvement. Long-term sustainability is prioritized along with outreach, education, and adaptation to local circumstances to handle challenges, including behavioral changes, initial expenses, and community collaboration.

The conservation practices may bring about a cultural change towards conservation, improved ecosystem health, resistance to climatic variability, and sustainable water management. Homesteaders have a critical role in creating a more sustainable and water-conscious future as they focus and improve their conservation efforts.

8.5 Sustainable Water Storage Solutions

The foundation of responsible homesteading water management is using sustainable water storage methods. This section delves into the importance, guiding principles, techniques, obstacles, and game-changing elements of implementing sustainable water storage solutions on the farm.

❖ **Importance of Ecological Water Storage Options:**

Providing Security for Water:

To guarantee water security on the homestead, sustainable water storage is essential. Homesteaders may lessen the effects of seasonal changes, droughts, or interruptions in the water supply by gathering and conserving water during times of excess. This proactive strategy adds to the homestead's resilience.

Agricultural Practices Supported:

A dependable water storage system helps agricultural activities by supplying irrigation with a steady water flow. This is especially crucial for homesteads engaged in sustainable agriculture since the time and availability of water may greatly impact crop yields and general production.

Being Ready for Emergencies:

Resilient water storage systems help people be ready for emergencies. Having water on hand guarantees that basic requirements, including drinking water and sanitation, may be satisfied when external water supplies are jeopardized. This makes the homestead more resilient to unanticipated difficulties.

❖ **Sustainable Water Storage Solutions' guiding principles:**

Making Capacity Plans:

The first step in efficiently storing water sustainably is capacity planning. Homesteaders evaluate their water demands, accounting for animal needs, irrigation needs, and home usage. The planning process directs the choice of storage systems with the right capacity to satisfy these requirements.

Combining Rainwater Harvesting and Integration:

Rainwater harvesting technologies and sustainable water storage are often integrated. Directly harvesting rainwater into storage tanks improves the homestead's capacity to catch and retain precipitation during rainy seasons and lessens dependency on other water sources.

Upkeep of Quality:

Preserving the quality of the water in storage systems is an essential idea. Homesteaders take precautions against contamination by establishing appropriate filtration systems, regularly cleaning storage tanks, and ensuring that the water stored is suitable for use in various applications.

Efficiency of Distribution:

Water distribution from storage systems must be done as efficiently as possible. Water is distributed throughout the homestead with the least amount of waste thanks to gravity-fed distribution systems, well-thought-out pipes, and well-placed outlets. This idea supports the more general objectives of water conservation.

❖ **Approaches to Ecological Water Storage Solutions:**

Systems for Harvesting Rainwater:

One of the main techniques for sustainable water storage is rainwater collection. Homesteaders divert rainfall into storage tanks by installing gutters and downspouts on their roofs. Rainwater may be collected and stored in these tanks — often furnished with filters — for various applications, such as domestic usage and irrigation.

Tanks and Cisterns:

Common infrastructure for sustainable water storage includes tanks and cisterns. Homesteaders may choose features that suit their requirements from various materials, sizes, and designs available for these vessels. Tanks and sterns are often positioned strategically to maximize water distribution and collecting.

Natural Reservoirs & Ponds:

Homesteaders may use ponds and other natural features or build reservoirs to store water. These may be incorporated into the landscape to promote biological variety and water storage. Considerations like evaporation management and ecological effects are part of proper design.

Systems for Recycling Greywater:

Systems for recycling greywater, which collects and cleans wastewater from domestic sources other than toilets, help ensure long-term water storage. Greywater may be saved for non-potable applications like irrigation after treatment, which lessens the strain on freshwater resources.

Effective Management:

Sustainable water storage for homesteads that depend on wells requires efficient, well management. Homesteaders monitor water levels, take precautions against overpumping, and ensure the well's production is sufficient for their purposes.

❖ **Difficulties with Sustainable Water Storage Methods:**

First Expenses:

Tanks, cisterns, and rainwater harvesting systems are examples of infrastructure with upfront expenses that make adopting sustainable water storage options difficult. Even though these expenditures have long-term advantages, some homesteaders may find the initial financial commitment a deterrent.

Sustaining Conditions:

For sustainable water storage systems to remain functional and long-lasting, constant maintenance is necessary. Continuous care is required for tank cleaning, leak detection, and water quality monitoring. Maintenance commitments may be difficult, particularly for homesteaders with hectic schedules.

Restricted Space for Storage:

Limited storage capacity may provide problems for homesteaders, especially during increased water demand or protracted dry spells. It takes careful planning and sometimes inventive solutions to balance the need for enough storage, available space, and budgetary restraints.

Variability in Climate:

Sustainable water storage is challenged by climate unpredictability. Homesteaders need to modify their storage systems to consider the possibility of longer or worse droughts and shifting precipitation patterns. This flexibility is essential to maintaining a steady supply of clean water.

❖ **Sustainable Water Storage Solutions' Transformative Aspects:**

Adaptability to Water Scarcity:

Sustainable water storage methods increase the homestead's resistance to water shortage. Homesteaders guarantee a steady water supply from outside sources even in times of scarcity by collecting and storing water during times of excess. This preventive strategy lessens the effects of interruptions or droughts.

Decreased Dependency and Self-Sufficiency:

Adopting environmentally friendly methods of storing water helps a country become self-sufficient. By lowering their reliance on outside water supplies, homesteaders have the independence to fulfill their water demands. This fits nicely with homesteading's larger philosophy of independence.

Increased Output in Agriculture:

Productivity in agriculture is significantly impacted by sustainable water storage. A stable water supply for irrigation promotes robust crop development, raising yields and promoting the sustainability of agriculture. This transforming element has special importance for homesteads that prioritize sustainable agriculture.

Secure Community Water Supply:

The community is impacted when sustainable water storage methods are put into practice. Homesteads can build resilience in the larger community by assisting with local water security. This integrated strategy demonstrates a shared accountability for long-term water resource management.

Finally, sustainable water storage options are essential to homesteading's ethical use of water resources. The concepts of capacity planning, integration with rainwater collecting, quality maintenance, and distribution efficiency guide the use of these technologies. Techniques include ponds, cisterns, rainwater collection systems, greywater recycling, and efficient well management. Careful planning and adaptation address upfront costs, maintenance requirements, limited storage capacity, and climate variability challenges.

The transformational characteristics of sustainable water storage technologies include better resistance to water shortage, self-sufficiency, improved agricultural output, and contributions to communal water security. As homesteaders continue to focus and enhance their water storage techniques, they contribute to a more sustainable and water-secure future.

Chapter 9: Community Building

9.1 The Importance of Community in Homesteading

Community is at the core of homesteading, which is essential in forming the experiences, resiliency, and collective wisdom of those seeking a sustainable way of life. The importance, guiding principles, techniques, difficulties, and transforming elements of creating and interacting with a homesteading community are examined in this section.

❖ **Community's Significance in Homesteading**

Mutual Assistance & Cooperation:

The camaraderie and cooperation that communities promote are crucial to homesteading. Homesteaders often encounter similar difficulties, and a vibrant community offers a network for sharing information, tools, and helpful advice. This team effort increases each homestead's resilience.

Cultural Diversity and Exchange:

Communities of homesteaders are often diverse because they include people with a range of backgrounds, abilities, and viewpoints. The community's cultural fabric is enhanced by this variety, which fosters an atmosphere in which many sustainable living philosophies may be discussed, honored, and gained knowledge.

Barter systems with shared resources:

Homesteading communities often create mechanisms for trading goods and services and exchanging resources. The capacity to trade commodities and services inside the community improves self-sufficiency and lessens the need for outside sources, whether surplus produce, skills, or equipment.

Workshops and Educational Initiatives:

Homesteading circles often provide seminars and community-based educational projects. These gatherings provide forums for information exchange, skill development, and advancing environmentally friendly behaviors. The community's cumulative knowledge becomes invaluable for novice and experienced homesteaders alike.

Getting Out of Isolation:

Particularly in rural places, homesteading may be a lonely endeavor. The community's social framework—companionship, shared experiences, and a feeling of belonging—fights loneliness. Breaking out from isolation has mental health benefits in addition to social ones.

❖ Homesteading's Community Building Principles:

Transparent Communication

One of the main tenets of homesteading community development is open and honest communication. Fulfilling confidence and cooperation entails freely exchanging ideas, problems, and experiences. Communication is facilitated via gatherings, online forums, and regular community meetings.

Courtesy toward diversity

One of the most important ideas is to respect and value variety. People in homesteading communities may come from diverse origins and adhere to distinct customs and beliefs. Building a culture that values and respects these distinctions makes a community rich and alive.

Mutual Exchange and Joint Accountability:

Two fundamental ideas are shared responsibility and reciprocity. Everyone in a homesteading community understands that they each have advantages and disadvantages. People give back to the community in proportion to their skills, and the community helps its members when needed.

Sustainability and Care of the Environment:

A common value among homesteading groups is environmental preservation. This calls for a group commitment to conservation initiatives, sustainable behaviors, and a shared responsibility for preserving the integrity of the surrounding environment.

Accessibility and Inclusivity:

It is essential to create a community that is accessible and inclusive. This entails setting up areas and activities that are friendly to people of all ages, skill levels, and backgrounds. A welcoming community makes the advantages of homesteading available to a diverse group of individuals.

❖ Homesteading Community Building Methodologies:

Collective Gardens and Common Areas:

In homesteading, communal spaces and gardens are useful strategies for fostering community. These areas provide a community place for socializing, seminars, and gardening. Community members' relationships are strengthened when they share maintenance and cultivation chores.

Web-based systems with social media:

Social media and internet platforms are important tools for homesteaders to develop communities in the digital era. Homesteaders, particularly those who may be geographically scattered, can communicate, share resources, and exchange ideas more easily when they use forums, organizations, and social media networks.

Workshops for Sharing Skills:

One efficient information transmission method in the community is to host skill-sharing workshops. These seminars promote a learning and skill development culture by imparting knowledge on everything from basic carpentry to gardening practices to food preservation methods.

Celebrations & Events in the Community:

Homesteading communities' social fabric is strengthened via gatherings and festivities. Residents may connect, exchange stories, and create a sense of community identity via gatherings for communal meals, harvest celebrations, and seasonal festivals.

Outreach & Involvement in the Community:

Participating in community outreach initiatives fosters relationships within the larger local community. Beyond the confines of their homestead, homesteaders may work with surrounding communities, participate in local activities, and support projects that support sustainable living.

Difficulties in Establishing a Community in Homesteading:

Regional Dispersion:

The geographical dispersion of homesteads is one of the difficulties associated with homesteading. Dispersed homesteads or remote areas might make it difficult to engage in physical contact regularly. Creative ways are needed to overcome this, such as planning centralized events or using digital communication.

Various Practices and Philosophies:

Communities that practice homesteading may face difficulties if their members have different beliefs or methods. A common commitment to the guiding principles of sustainability, as well as candid communication and compromise, is necessary to balance individual liberty and group objectives.

Constrained Resources

Building communities might be difficult when there aren't enough material or financial resources. Investment may be needed for shared space creation, event planning, and community project execution. Overcoming these restrictions requires the ingenuity and resourcefulness of the community.

Time Restrictions:

Time limits may provide a problem in community development since homesteaders often manage numerous duties. Effective time management and prioritizing are necessary to balance running a homestead and engaging in community involvement.

The Changing Character of Homesteading Community Building:

Mutual Aid and Resilience:

Through reciprocal assistance, community formation in homesteading promotes resilience. When faced with difficulties, whether natural catastrophes or human tragedies, the community joins as a source of support. The power resulting from group resilience and the capacity to face hardship together is transformational.

Learning and Enrichment via Culture:

Creating a varied community enhances homesteading's cultural fabric. Sharing customs, ideas, and practices promotes lifelong learning and cultural enrichment. This transformational feature emphasizes how homesteading communities are dynamic and ever-changing.

The combined effect on regional sustainability:

The collaborative efforts of homesteading communities greatly impact local sustainability. The transformational element is the community's influence upon more general sustainable practices in the surrounding area, from cooperative conservation initiatives to community-supported agriculture.

Mental Health and Relationships:

Their feeling of belonging and community greatly enhances homesteaders' mental health. Having a support system, sharing experiences, and overcoming loneliness all have a favorable effect on mental health. The transforming element is the change from possible solitude to a feeling of connection and belonging.

In summary, the significance of community in homesteading cannot be overstated, as it shapes the shared knowledge, experiences, and resilience of those who strive for a sustainable way of life — the values of transparency, inclusion, sustainability, reciprocity, and respect for diversity guide community development. Community gardens, online forums, seminars for skill-sharing, events, and outreach are examples of methodologies. Obstacles like geographical separation, conflicting ideologies, resource scarcity, and schedule limitations are overcome with imagination and dedication.

Resilience via mutual help, cultural enrichment, group influence on regional sustainability, and beneficial contributions to mental health are some transforming elements. Homesteading communities are examples of how group efforts may build a more connected and sustainable way of life as they develop further.

9.2 Networking with Like-minded Individuals

Building a community by networking with like-minded people is essential to homesteading because it offers a forum for information sharing, cooperation, and sharing common ideals. The importance, guiding principles, techniques, obstacles, and revolutionary elements of networking in the homesteading community are examined in this section.

❖ **Networking Is Important for Homesteading:**

Common Purposes and Ideals:

In homesteading, networking with like-minded people is important since these relationships are based on common ideals and objectives. People interested in living a self-sufficient, sustainable lifestyle are similarly dedicated to environmental protection, resilience, and a desire to live near the earth.

Knowledge Transfer:

A wide range of abilities and methods are needed for homesteading, and networking offers a forum for information sharing. Homesteaders may enhance their skills and capacities by tapping into the collective knowledge of a network, which can be used for everything from animal husbandry to renewable energy and organic farming.

Collective Initiatives:

Networking enables homesteaders to work together on projects. Like-minded people may combine money, talents, and energies to work on projects that benefit the whole community, from shared infrastructure initiatives to communal gardens. This cooperative mindset improves individual homesteads' sustainability and self-sufficiency.

Community Adaptability:

A network of people who share similar values strengthens community resilience during difficult times, whether brought on by inclement weather, shifting economic conditions, or other unanticipated occurrences. The network's mutual assistance and pooled resources help homesteaders better withstand adversity and adjust to shifting circumstances.

Promoting Creativity:

Within the homesteading community, networking promotes creativity. Through interacting with others who possess a variety of viewpoints and life experiences, homesteaders might discover novel concepts, methods, and environmentally friendly behaviors. The constant stream of invention adds to homesteading's adaptable and dynamic character.

❖ **Guidelines for Connecting with Like-Minded People:**

Common Ethics and Values:

Homesteading networking is built based on common ideals and values. People who value self-sufficiency, environmental sustainability, and a holistic way of life are united by a shared ethos. These common values serve as the foundation for trust and cooperation in networking.

Honesty and Cooperation:

A fundamental idea of networking is being willing to work together. Homesteaders freely share their resources, expertise, and experiences because they understand the advantages of teamwork. This idea promotes a cooperative rather than a competitive attitude, creating a cohesive and supportive society.

Regard for Personal Decisions:

Respect for personal preferences is a guiding concept in networking, even if it is founded on common principles. Homesteaders in a network know that every person's homesteading experience is different and that different strategies may succeed. Respect for personal preferences fosters an accepting and nonjudgmental community.

Mutual Aid and Reciprocity:

Networking with like-minded people is based on the basic concepts of reciprocity and mutual help. Homesteaders in the network share resources, lend a hand and give help when needed, all of which enhance the community's well-being. An adaptable network's core is its reciprocal interaction.

Diversity and Inclusivity:

Networking in homesteading is guided by the values of inclusivity and celebrating diversity. A network that accepts people with different experiences, backgrounds, and viewpoints fosters a lively and dynamic community. The network can benefit from various perspectives, abilities, and cultural influences by being inclusive.

❖ **Techniques for Connecting with Like-Minded People:**

Regional Homesteading Associations:

Local homesteading associations are good sources of networking information. These organizations often plan frequent get-togethers, seminars, and events so that people with similar interests can interact, exchange stories, and collaborate on initiatives. Local organizations develop intimate relationships and a smaller-scale sense of community.

Forums and Platforms Online:

Online platforms and forums are a major part of networking in the digital era. People may interact with each other worldwide via homesteading-related websites, social media groups, and forums. These platforms make it easier to solve problems, share ideas, and forge connections across geographical divides.

Initiatives and Projects for Collaboration:

Initiatives and collaborative projects are useful networking techniques. Collaborative projects, such as a shared workshop space, a community garden, or a renewable energy initiative, unite like-minded people to work toward shared objectives. These initiatives reinforce the ties within the network.

Conferences and Events on Homesteading:

Like-minded people get together for homesteading conferences and gatherings. Participants may attend classes, network, and participate in conversations on sustainable living. These gatherings provide a great setting for networking and growing one's homesteading network.

Casual Get-Togethers and Potlucks:

Potlucks and casual get-togethers provide a laid-back environment for networking. Homesteaders might have informal get-togethers to exchange ideas, tales, and food. The social fiber of the homesteading community is strengthened in these casual situations, which promote genuine relationships.

❖ **Difficulties in Forming Networks with Like-Minded People:**

Geographical Obstacles:

Geographical boundaries are one of the problems when networking with like-minded folks. Since homesteaders may live far apart, regularly communicating in person might be difficult. Utilizing digital platforms with local networking is necessary to overcome this obstacle.

Various Methods for Homesteading:

Various homesteading methods might cause problems in a network. People could differ in their ideas, tastes, and degrees of independence. Finding common ground while navigating these differences calls for honest communication, tolerance for variety, and an emphasis on shared values.

Time Restrictions:

Networking may be difficult when pressed for time, particularly for homesteaders who have a lot on their plates daily. Effective time management and prioritizing are necessary to balance the demands of the homestead and active involvement in a network.

Restrictions on Resources:

Resource constraints may impact networking initiatives, whether monetary or related to the availability of tools and equipment. Collaborative initiatives may encounter difficulties if participants do not have the required resources. Innovative solutions and an emphasis on network resource sharing are needed to overcome these obstacles.

❖ **The Changing Benefits of Connecting with Like-Minded People:**

Knowledge Expansion:

Building a network with like-minded people increases knowledge among homesteaders. The network's collective expertise develops into a potent resource that enhances each person's habits, skills, and capacity for problem-solving. This transformational element supports ongoing education and development.

Increased Prospects for Cooperation:

Collaboration possibilities increase with networking. Homesteaders provide opportunities for joint ventures, resource sharing, and cooperative projects by establishing connections with various people. This transformational element improves the community of homesteaders' sustainability and self-sufficiency.

Cultural Enrichment and Exchange:

Networking makes it easier for the homesteading community to enhance and share cultures. People from various locations, experiences, and backgrounds provide distinctive viewpoints to the network. Because of this variety, there is a more vibrant cross-cultural interchange and a broader knowledge of sustainable living.

Enhanced Support and Resilience:

Networking may be revolutionary since it increases resilience and support. A support system of like-minded people offers a safety net in trying times. The network improves homesteaders' general resilience and well-being by providing emotional support and resource sharing amid shortages.

In summary, networking with like-minded people is an important part of creating a community when homesteading since it presents chances for cooperation, information sharing, and shared ideals. Examples of networking approaches include local organizations, internet platforms, cooperative initiatives, conferences, and casual get-togethers. These are all based on inclusion, openness, respect, and reciprocity. Obstacles like distance, divergent methods, time limits, and resource scarcity are overcome by developing innovative solutions and keeping the common objectives front and center.

Transformational networking elements include knowledge amplification, more chances for cooperation, cultural enrichment and exchange, and heightened resilience and support. Homesteaders contribute to a vibrant, linked community dedicated to sustainable living as they continue to form connections and networks.

9.3 Shared Resources and Barter Systems

In homesteading, barter systems and shared resources are essential for community formation. This section delves into the importance, guiding principles, techniques, obstacles, and transforming elements of resource sharing and bartering among homesteaders.

The Importance of Barter Systems and Shared Resources in Homesteading:

Interdependence and Mutual Assistance:

Homesteading communities are built based on mutual support and interdependence via shared resources and barter systems. The capacity to share tools, equipment, and talents promotes a feeling of community in a lifestyle that emphasizes sustainability and self-sufficiency, where people depend on one another for their overall well-being.

Diminution of Personal Expenses:

Homesteading often entails high upfront and continuing expenses. By combining their resources, homesteaders may lower their expenses thanks to shared resources. Sustainable living may be more economically feasible if homesteaders jointly owned and maintained these resources rather than each purchasing pricey tools or equipment individually.

Improved Independence:

Bartering and resource sharing make homesteaders more self-sufficient. Homesteaders lessen their need for outside markets and suppliers by trading products and services inside the community. This approach is consistent with the fundamental resilience and sustainability concepts found in homesteading.

Constructing an Adaptive Community:

Barter systems and shared resources help to create a robust homesteading community. The community's capacity to pool resources and lean on one another during trying times, whether brought on by external circumstances, economic changes, or individual disappointments, enhances its resilience. The foundation of a healthy community is this interconnectivity.

❖ **Shared Resource and Barter System Principles:**

Confidence and Equivalency:

Shared resources and barter systems are based on the fundamental concepts of reciprocity and trust. Homesteaders in the community must have faith that resources will be distributed equitably and that barter trades will be built on reciprocal connections. This trust fosters collaboration and a feeling of security.

A Fair Distribution

A guiding concept to guarantee that pooled resources benefit every community member is equitable distribution. A spirit of equality among homesteaders should be promoted by the equitable and open allocation of resources, whether tools, a greenhouse, or common storage facilities.

Unambiguous Communication

In systems based on shared resources and barter, effective communication is essential. It is important for homesteaders to proficiently convey their requirements, resource accessibility, and barter agreements' conditions. This clarity guarantees that everyone in the community has access to the resources they need and lessens the possibility of misunderstandings.

Adaptability and Flexibility:

Principles of adaptation and flexibility are crucial in barter and shared resource systems. Communities of homesteaders are dynamic, their needs and circumstances ever-changing. These systems' sustained sustainability depends on their capacity to adjust to changing circumstances and be accommodating in resource-sharing arrangements.

Respect toward personal autonomy

Even though barter systems and shared resources need group collaboration, upholding individual autonomy is a fundamental value. Homesteaders are still in charge of how they utilize resources and make decisions. Respect for one another allows people to pursue their homesteading objectives and benefit from common resources.

❖ **Techniques for Barter Systems and Shared Resources:**

Tool Collections and Equipment Cooperatives:

Cooperatives for equipment and tool libraries are useful strategies for pooling resources. These projects include building a shared tool and equipment library that homesteaders can use as required. This guarantees the effective use of resources and lessens the financial strain on individual homesteaders.

Shared Harvests and Community Gardens:

Two ways to share agricultural resources are via community gardens and shared harvests. Homesteaders cultivate and enjoy the benefits of a communal garden, sharing the product. Through shared effort and bounty, this not only makes fresh, locally farmed food accessible, but it also strengthens the feeling of community.

Workshops for Sharing Skills and Time Banks:

Methodologies for barter systems include time banks and skill-sharing seminars. Homesteaders share their experiences and impart useful talents to one another via skill-sharing. By exchanging work hours or services, time banks provide a system in which people give according to their skills and get help.

Plant and Seed Exchanges:

Plant and seed exchanges are two ways agricultural resources are shared in homesteading communities. By trading seeds, seedlings, or existing plants, homesteaders increase the diversity of crops cultivated in their community. This encourages resilience, biodiversity, and community involvement in agriculture.

Typical Storage Locations:

Sharing resources like bulk purchases of food, seeds, or equipment makes sense by using common storage facilities. Together, homesteaders may buy and store goods in a common area, saving money on individual expenses and guaranteeing everyone in the community can access necessary supplies.

❖ **Problems with Barter Systems and Shared Resources:**

Differential Contribution

An issue with barter and shared resource systems is the possibility of uneven participation. Feelings of imbalance or anger may arise in the community if some members give more to the pooled resources or trade more often. It will need open communication and a dedication to fair participation to address this situation.

Upkeep of Resources and Accountability:

Shared resource maintenance calls for accountability and collaboration. It isn't easy to ensure that everyone in the community assumes their fair share of maintaining tools, equipment, or common areas. To solve this issue, precise maintenance criteria must be established.

Handling Conflicts:

Shared resource and barter systems may lead to conflicts, particularly when miscommunications or varying expectations exist. Effective conflict resolution techniques are essential for homesteaders to handle disputes and guarantee that barter agreements and shared resources improve community relations.

Managing Independence and Cooperation:

It might be difficult to strike the correct balance between individual freedom and teamwork. Homesteaders may range widely in their level of self-sufficiency. Therefore, it takes skill to navigate shared resources and barter systems such that they respect individual liberty while encouraging communal cooperation.

Durability of Barter Systems:

Barter arrangements could run into sustainability issues. Barter systems may lose their effectiveness if the conditions of trade are unclear or if the requirements of the community change. To meet this difficulty, barter agreements must be regularly reviewed and modified.

❖ **Barter systems and shared resources: transformative aspects**

Developing a Feeling of Community:

A strong feeling of community is fostered via barter systems and shared resources. A web of interdependence is formed when homesteaders actively contribute to and profit from shared resources. This transforming element fosters a community where people cooperate for the well-being of everyone, strengthening the social fabric.

Encouragement of Environmental Care:

The shared use of resources is consistent with environmental stewardship ideals. Homesteaders support a more sustainable lifestyle by sharing tools or equipment and lowering individual use. This revolutionary feature demonstrates a dedication to conservation and wise resource usage.

Improving Community and Individual Resilience:

Resilience on the individual and communal levels is increased via barter systems and shared resources. The community's collective strength is enhanced by the capacity to depend on one another for resources, expertise, and assistance when things go tough. This transformational element shows how adaptable and successful we can all be as a group.

Promoting Creativity and Resourcefulness:

Within the community, barter systems and shared resources foster creativity and ingenuity. Homesteaders may develop original ideas, exchange fresh perspectives, and investigate different methods for leading sustainable lives. This transforming element supports a vibrant and changing homesteading community.

Creating a Reciprocal Culture:

Creating a reciprocity-based culture is the transforming element of barter systems and shared resources. As a result of their active give-and-take interactions, homesteaders actively promote mutual trust and support. This culture becomes a motivating factor in community dynamics, influencing how people communicate and work together.

To sum up, barter systems and shared resources are essential to homesteading communities because they promote cooperation, lower personal expenses, and increase self-sufficiency. Techniques include tool libraries, community gardens, skill-sharing seminars, and shared storage facilities. The values of trust, equal distribution, open communication, flexibility, and respect for individual autonomy underpin them. Careful consideration is needed to address issues including uneven contribution, resource upkeep, dispute resolution, autonomy balance, and the sustainability of barter arrangements.

A culture of reciprocity, resilience, creativity, shared resources, and environmental stewardship are just a few of the transformational effects of barter and shared resources systems. Homesteaders help build a vibrant, connected community dedicated to sustainable living by actively participating in shared resource and barter projects.

9.4 Educational Initiatives and Workshops

A key component of the homesteading lifestyle is community development, which is achieved via educational programs and seminars. The importance, guiding principles, techniques, obstacles, and transforming elements of educational programs and seminars in homesteading communities are explored in this section.

❖ **The Importance of Workshops and Educational Initiatives:**

Exchange of Knowledge and Development of Skills:

Education programs and seminars are essential in homesteading communities because they promote skill development and knowledge exchange. Homesteaders gather to exchange knowledge, learn new skills, and broaden their awareness of sustainable living techniques. This common understanding enhances the community's resilience and self-sufficiency.

Developing the Community's Members:

Through the provision of necessary equipment and information, these projects enable community members to live self-sustainable lifestyles. People feel more empowered in the community as they grow more proficient in different homesteading skills, which boosts their confidence and ability to make wise judgments.

Creating a Community of Learning:

Workshops and educational activities aid in the development of a learning community. Homesteaders participate in an ongoing process of mutual learning, encouraging curiosity and inspiring people to try out novel concepts and methods. A dynamic feature of the homesteading way of life is this learning culture.

Cultural Guardianship:

Preserving traditional knowledge and skills relevant to sustainable living is typically part of homesteading. Workshops and educational programs serve as a vehicle for preserving culture by transferring important customs from generation to generation. This keeps the homesteading community's ties to its history and origins strong.

❖ **The Fundamentals of Workshops and Educational Initiatives:**

Inclusivity and Accessibility:

In homesteading communities, inclusiveness and accessibility serve as guiding principles for educational endeavors. To ensure that everyone can participate and gain from the learning opportunities, workshops should suit persons with different expertise and resources.

Active Learning:

A key tenet of homesteading education programs is experiential learning. Attendees may actively participate in homesteading activities during workshops, often including hands-on, experiential learning. This practical approach improves the development of practical skills and the retention of information.

Community-Based Learning:

The concept that each person in the homesteading community has important information to impart is emphasized by community-led education. This idea promotes a decentralized method of education in which community members alternately teach seminars according to their areas of competence. This encourages cooperation and a feeling of shared responsibility for schooling.

Ability to Adjust to Community Needs:

Educational programs must be flexible enough to meet the community's changing demands. This concept acknowledges the dynamic nature of homesteading communities, characterized by shifting problems and interests. Workshops must adapt to these shifts by providing timely and relevant information for the community's requirements.

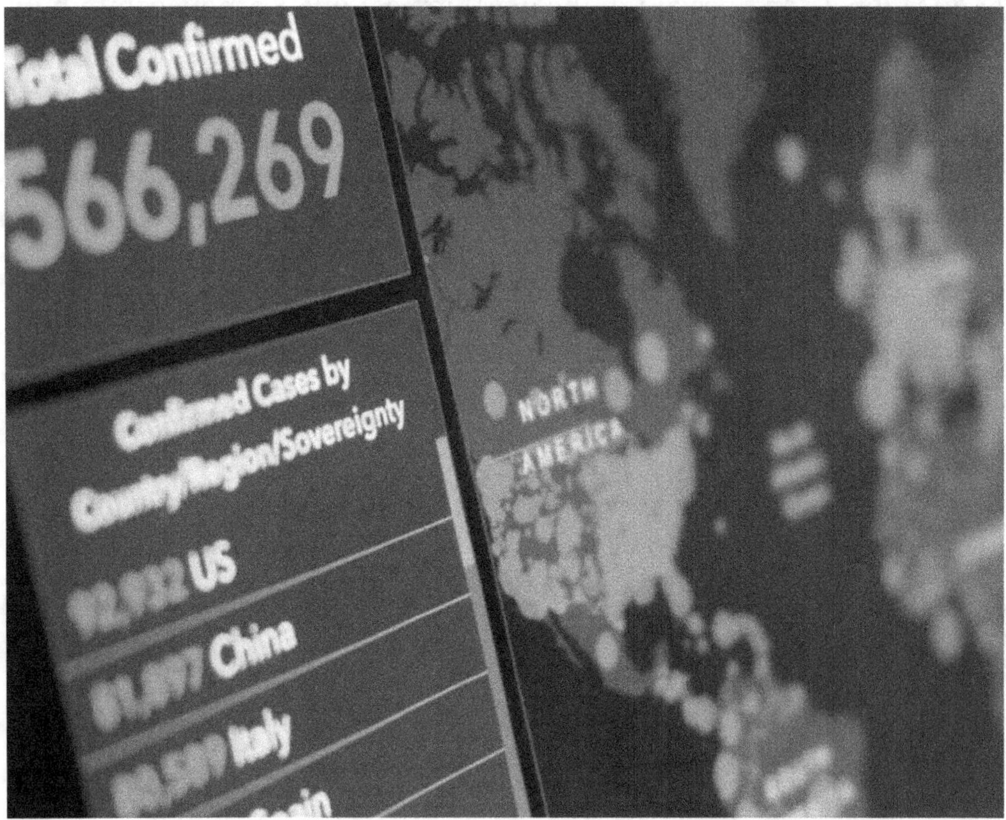

Lifelong Education:

In homesteading communities, the value of lifelong learning is paramount. The premise is that education is a lifelong process that should not be limited to a certain age or stage. This approach promotes people to be lifelong learners, receptive to new concepts, and dedicated to their development.

❖ **Approaches to Educational Projects and Workshops:**

Expert-Related Workshops:

Workshops designed to teach certain homesteading techniques or skills are called skill-specific workshops. These classes may address everything from woodworking and food preservation to organic gardening and animal husbandry. Depending on their interests and desired skill set, participants may choose workshops.

Workshops with a seasonal and theme focus:

Workshops that are themed and seasonal are designed to meet homesteading communities' changing requirements and goals. Seasonally appropriate topics for a workshop can include winter preparation or spring planting. Workshops with a theme might delve into certain facets of homesteading, including sustainable construction techniques or renewable energy.

Experts and Visiting Instructors:

Visiting lecturers and specialists is a technique that enhances learning programs. Homesteading groups might invite experts to provide in-depth information or conduct courses on advanced subjects. This method offers a variety of viewpoints and expands the breadth of learning.

Community Partnerships:

Community collaborations are an effective approach. Members with specialized knowledge in different areas may work together to provide in-depth courses covering various homesteading topics. This cooperative strategy fosters a feeling of solidarity and group accountability for education.

Online Education Resources:

Online learning environments help educational endeavors reach a wider audience in the digital era. Homesteaders may communicate virtually via webinars, online courses, and workshops, overcoming geographical limitations. This approach takes into account a range of remote learning preferences and timetables.

❖ **Difficulties with Educational Programs and Workshops:**

Restrictions on Resources:

Resource limitations, including a lack of money or specialized tools, might make planning educational programs difficult. Homesteading groups need to develop innovative ways to get beyond these limitations, such as pooling resources or enlisting outside help.

Variation in Skill Levels:

People in homesteading communities may have different backgrounds and specializations. Creating workshops accommodating the community's wide range of skill levels might be difficult. Careful preparation is needed to ensure the material is balanced to suit novice and seasoned homesteaders.

Setting Up and Devoting Time:

Time commitments and scheduling may be difficult, particularly in communities where people have hectic schedules or seasonal obligations. Coordination and adaptability are needed to find workshop times that work for everyone and to accommodate varying availability.

Successful Interaction:

For educational endeavors to be successful, effective communication is essential. Clear communication regarding workshop scheduling, content, and expectations is necessary to ensure that community members can participate completely in the learning process. Misunderstandings and decreased involvement may result from poor communication.

Harmonizing Innovation with Tradition:

It may not be easy to balance tradition and innovation, particularly when dealing with different viewpoints within the community. While some members may favor more conventional approaches, others may welcome contemporary advancements. Initiatives in education must find a middle ground that honors both perspectives and promotes peaceful cohabitation.

❖ **Educational Initiatives and Workshops' Transformative Aspects:**

Self-determination and assurance:

Education programs provide people in the community with a feeling of empowerment and self-efficacy. Individuals get more confident in their capacity to overcome the difficulties of homesteading as they pick up new abilities and information. Through empowerment, people become competent and proactive members of the community.

Socially cohesive culture:

A coherent community culture is developed via involvement in educational projects. Community members form relationships via shared learning experiences, which promote cohesion and shared identity. This transforming element strengthens the homesteading community's social fabric.

Inventiveness and Flexibility:

Homesteading communities are encouraged to be innovative and adaptable via educational efforts. People experimenting and acquiring new skills help the community become more flexible in response to changing conditions. This transformational feature promotes a resilient and ever-improving culture.

Maintaining Conventional Wisdom:

One transforming result of educational programs is the preservation of traditional knowledge. The transmission of cultural legacy to future generations is ensured by workshops that concentrate on traditional homesteading methods. Its preservation strengthens the community's ties to its heritage.

Mindset for Lifelong Learning:

Participating in educational programs fosters an attitude of continuous learning among homesteaders. The transformation goes beyond particular programs to a shared commitment to lifelong learning. This kind of thinking becomes a motivator for individual and group development.

In short, community formation in homesteading is greatly aided by educational programs and seminars. These programs support empowerment, skill development, knowledge exchange, and cultural heritage preservation. Online learning platforms, skill-specific workshops, seasonal and theme-based workshops, guest instructors, community collaborations, hands-on learning, accessibility, and community-led education serve as guiding principles for these techniques. Careful care must be given to issues with limited resources, a range of skill levels, scheduling, efficient communication, and striking a balance between tradition and innovation.

Educational efforts that foster empowerment, a cohesive community culture, innovation, preserving traditional knowledge, and developing a lifelong learning attitude are considered transformational. Homesteaders help to build a resilient, powerful, and dynamic community dedicated to sustainable living by actively participating in educational programs.

9.5 Overcoming Isolation: Creating a Supportive Homesteading Community

One of the most common obstacles to pursuing a homesteading lifestyle is the possibility of loneliness. A feeling of isolation may result from homesteading's expansive vistas and self-sufficient lifestyle. This section delves into the importance, guiding principles, techniques, obstacles, and transforming elements involved in establishing a supportive homesteading community that aids in overcoming loneliness.

❖ **The Importance of Establishing a Community of Supportive Homesteaders:**

Practical and Emotional Assistance:

A homesteading community's emotional and practical support makes it so important. Homesteaders often have particular difficulties, such as handling severe weather and maintaining sustainable practices. A close-knit community provides a network of people aware of these difficulties and can give practical answers and emotional support.

Pooled Resources and Information:

Fostering a network of support facilitates the exchange of information and resources. A community may pool its resources to ensure that individual homesteaders have access to a wider variety of resources and abilities, whether they are tools, seeds, or knowledge of particular homesteading techniques.

Building Community Resilience:

Collective resilience is fostered in a homesteading community that is supportive. During unforeseen obstacles or failures, community members may rely on one another, exchange stories, and work together to overcome challenging circumstances. The sustainability of the community as a whole is based on this shared resilience.

Reduction of Stress Associated with Isolation:

Feelings of loneliness and stress may both be exacerbated by isolation. A caring homesteading community reduces these pressures by fostering a sense of community, shared obligations, and social connections. Homesteaders benefit emotionally by belonging to a community that respects and appreciates their way of life.

❖ **Guidelines for Establishing a Helpful Homesteading Community:**

Broadcasting and Transparency:

Openness and inclusivity are fundamental ideas in building a community that is encouraging. Communities practicing homesteading must welcome people with various experiences, backgrounds, and abilities. All community members are encouraged to participate in events actively and feel a feeling of belonging in an open and inclusive environment.

Mutual Honor and Collaboration:

Two fundamental elements of a cooperative homesteading community are mutual respect and collaboration. Every community member contributes special talents and viewpoints, and an atmosphere of collaboration is fostered by acknowledging and appreciating these differences. The community's fabric is strengthened when members work together to achieve shared objectives.

Successful Interaction:

Overcoming isolation may be facilitated by practicing effective communication. Community members are aware of one other's needs, difficulties, and efforts when there is open and transparent communication between them. Open communication promotes cooperative problem-solving within the community and helps to establish trust.

Joint Accountability:

To have a supportive homesteading community, shared duties are essential. By assigning duties and obligations to community members, the load is distributed among them, and a spirit of teamwork is fostered. This idea encourages a shared commitment and reciprocal culture.

Encouragement of Personal Independence:

As important as teamwork is, fostering individual liberty should equally be a guiding concept. A homesteading community's members must be allowed to follow their dreams and objectives. Each person's efforts are recognized and rewarded when autonomy and teamwork are balanced.

❖ **Techniques for Establishing a Helping Homesteading Community:**

Often Occurring Community Events:

Frequent neighborhood get-togethers provide chances for conversation and social engagement. Weekly meetings, workdays, or seasonal festivities—all of these get-togethers contribute to the homesteaders' feeling of community and personal relationships.

Internet forums and platforms:

Online communities and platforms allow homesteaders to communicate virtually in the digital era. Information, guidance, and assistance may be shared in virtual places. People may discuss their experiences and ask others going through similar things for advice in online forums.

Skill-Transfer Programs:

Initiatives to share skills foster a culture of knowledge exchange in the community. People may impart knowledge and gain insights from one another via workshops, training sessions, or casual skill-sharing gatherings. This approach improves the community's collective skill set and fortifies the ties among its constituents.

Community Initiatives and Partnerships:

Homesteaders get together for common goals via community initiatives and partnerships. Building community buildings, tending a community garden, or implementing sustainable ideas are just a few examples of cooperative undertakings that foster a feeling of cohesion and purpose among neighbors.

Creation of Support Systems:

More personal relationships may be made via support networks and smaller community organizations. These groups may concentrate on particular hobbies, difficulties, or objectives. By creating support networks, each participant may be certain they have a close-knit support system for guidance, help, and company.

❖ **Difficulties in Establishing a Helping Homesteading Community:**

Regional Seclusion:

A big obstacle to building a strong homesteading community is geographic remoteness. Since homesteaders may be dispersed across great distances, getting together regularly might be difficult. To overcome this obstacle, innovative ideas are needed, including setting up online gatherings or creating local clusters.

Diversity in Attitudes and Ways of Life:

Although it may be enlightening, diversity in the community can often provide difficulties. Conflicts may arise from disparities in ideals, lifestyles, and homesteading techniques. Finding common ground that brings the community together, being open in communication, and being committed to understanding other points of view are all necessary to address these disparities.

Restrictions on Resources:

Limitations in resources, including time, money, or skills accessible, might impede the development of a community that is supportive. Someack the means may take an active role in community events. Inclusion requires using solutions that account for different degrees of resource availability.

Participation and Engagement in the Community:

Participation and community involvement may be difficult, particularly if some members want a more secluded homesteading lifestyle. Promoting the advantages of community involvement while also honoring individual decisions to encourage active participation without placing expectations takes a delicate balance.

Taking Charge and Making Decisions:

Making decisions and exercising leadership may be difficult, especially when no defined procedures exist. It is possible to foster an inclusive society where no one feels excluded by ensuring that leadership positions are alternated, decisions are made cooperatively, and everyone's opinions are appreciated.

❖ **Revolutionary Features of Establishing a Helpful Homesteading Community:**

The feeling of Acceptance:

A strong sense of community is fostered by building a supportive homesteading community. Homesteaders have a sense of community with like-minded people who appreciate the nuances of their way of life and share their ideals. This common identity and emotional stability that come from belonging are transformational.

Collaborative Issue-Solving:

Difficulties become chances for group problem-solving in a supportive community. Homesteaders may use the many viewpoints and skill sets present in the community to create creative solutions when confronted with challenges. The community as a whole becomes more resilient because of this cooperative approach to problem-solving.

Cultural Communication and Education:

A friendly homesteading community fosters transformational features via cultural exchange and learning. Members can gain knowledge from one another's homesteading methods, customs, and cultural backgrounds. Individual viewpoints are widened by this enlightening experience, which also builds a more welcoming and culturally varied community.

Improved Emotional Health:

Homesteaders' mental health is improved when they can overcome their isolation with the help of their community. The lowered stress and loneliness levels are clear indicators of the transformational effect. Community members' emotional support fosters a supportive and loving atmosphere that enhances mental health and well-being in general.

Joint Accomplishments and Festivities:

A friendly homesteading community leads to accomplishments and festivities that everybody enjoys. Whether it's harvesting a bountiful crop, finishing a group project, or hitting sustainability benchmarks, these mutually satisfying events strengthen the ties in the community. A feeling of satisfaction and accomplishment is generated when accomplishments are celebrated together.

In summary, building a network of supporting homesteaders and overcoming isolation is essential to the prosperity and well-being of homesteaders. The importance is in providing practical and emotional support, pooling resources, building group resilience, and reducing stress from isolation. Guided by principles of inclusivity, mutual respect, effective communication, shared responsibilities, and encouragement of individual autonomy, methodologies include regular community gatherings, online platforms, skill-sharing initiatives, community projects, and support networks.

Challenges related to geographical isolation, diversity of lifestyles, resource limitations, community engagement, and leadership require thoughtful consideration. The transformative aspects include a sense of belonging, collective problem-solving, cultural exchange and learning, enhanced emotional well-being, and shared achievements and celebrations. As homesteaders actively create and sustain a supportive community, they contribute to a resilient, connected, and thriving collective committed to the principles of sustainable living.

Chapter 10: Challenges and Solutions

10.1 Dealing with Unforeseen Challenges

With its emphasis on sustainability and self-sufficiency, homesteading is difficult. This section explores the importance, guiding concepts, approaches, difficulties, and life-changing elements of overcoming unanticipated obstacles in the homesteading lifestyle.

❖ **The Importance of Overcoming Unexpected Difficulties:**

The Adaptive Character of Homesteading

Because homesteading is such a dynamic lifestyle, it is important to cope with unanticipated obstacles. Unexpected challenges are common for homesteaders, including erratic weather patterns, severe crop illnesses, and unanticipated economic changes. A homestead's capacity to survive and prosper depends on its ability to overcome these obstacles.

Adaptivity and Resilience:

The homesteading community develops resilience and adaptation by overcoming unanticipated hurdles. Effective homesteaders show they can recover from unforeseen failures, grow from them, and modify their methods. A homestead's long-term survival depends on its capacity to withstand setbacks.

Stopping the Escalation:

Dealing with problems early on stops them from becoming bigger problems. Homesteaders may lessen the effects of difficulties before they become too great by planning unanticipated events and having contingency plans. Proactive tactics enhance the overall stability and durability of the homesteading attempt.

Ongoing Education and Development:

The importance of overcoming obstacles extends to the community of homesteaders' ongoing education and development. Every unexpected obstacle presents a chance for development and learning. Homesteaders support a culture of continual improvement by examining the underlying causes of problems and coming up with workable solutions.

❖ **Guidelines for Handling Unexpected Difficulties:**

Anticipatory Planning:

One of the main ideas for handling unanticipated difficulties is proactive preparation. Homesteaders must prepare for unforeseen circumstances and foresee possible hazards. This idea promotes a proactive strategy in which the community is ready for various eventualities, even ones that may seem improbable initially.

Working Together to Solve Problems:

The guiding concept of collaborative problem-solving stresses teamwork in overcoming obstacles. Within a community, homesteaders contribute a variety of abilities and viewpoints. The community leverages its combined creativity and intellect through collaborative problem-solving and analysis.

Adaptability and Flexibility:

Adaptability and flexibility are fundamental ideas for handling unanticipated difficulties. Homesteaders must be flexible enough to modify their strategies and plans in response to changing conditions. This approach promotes an open-minded attitude and the readiness to change course.

Constant Observation and Assessment:

The guiding principles of continuous monitoring and assessment encourage vigilance in evaluating the homestead's state. Homesteaders may identify such problems early on and take prompt action by routinely assessing the well-being of their animals, crops, and general sustainability practices.

Making Use of Experience

The idea of learning from experience acknowledges obstacles as worthwhile chances for growth. Homesteaders see losses as opportunities to improve their methods and strengthen their resilience rather than seeing them as failures. This idea promotes a growth attitude and a dedication to continuous development.

❖ **Strategies for Overcoming Unexpected Obstacles:**

Evaluation and mitigation of risks:

The process of conducting risk assessments includes recognizing possible obstacles and implementing plans to lessen their effects. This proactive strategy lessens the possibility of unanticipated difficulties producing major disruptions by enabling homesteaders to plan and anticipate a variety of eventualities.

Plans for Emergency Preparedness:

Creating emergency plans is a process that provides a list of steps to follow in case of unanticipated difficulties. Protocols for severe weather, agricultural diseases, and economic downturns could be included in these strategies. Well-defined and communicated plans guarantee a prompt and coordinated reaction in the event of difficulties.

Workshops & Training for the Community:

Community seminars and training sessions provide homesteaders with the expertise required to tackle problems as a group. These seminars may address everything from financial preparedness for difficult economic times to agricultural methods resistant to weather. Increasing a community's common knowledge makes it more resilient to adversity.

Networks for exchanging information:

Creating networks for information exchange is a strategy that helps homesteaders be aware of impending difficulties. Exchanges of illness warnings, market trends, and weather predictions may occur over these networks. Prompt knowledge enables homesteaders to address new difficulties and make well-informed judgments proactively.

Protocols for Crisis Communication:

Creating crisis communication protocols is a process that guarantees efficient communication in the face of unanticipated difficulties. Establishing and maintaining clear lines of communication and procedures facilitates prompt information dissemination, response coordination, and community awareness of the issue and any required actions.

❖ **Difficulties of Overcoming Unexpected Obstacles:**

Constrained Resources

Having few financial, material, or human resources can make it difficult to handle unanticipated difficulties. Homesteaders may have difficulties putting emergency preparations into action or obtaining the necessary equipment and supplies. Overcoming this obstacle requires developing systems for sharing resources and developing innovative solutions.

The intricacy of Networked Systems:

Because homesteading includes interrelated systems, solving one problem might have unintended consequences for other ones. Because of the intricate nature of these relationships, it may not be easy to foresee every possible result. It takes thoughtful thought and flexibility to respond to obstacles in a way that doesn't lead to new issues.

Stress Psychological:

Homesteaders may experience psychological stress when they have to deal with unanticipated obstacles. Anxiety and emotional distress might result from the uncertainty and possible effects on livelihoods. Creating an encouraging, friendly community that offers emotional support is essential to reducing psychological stress.

Outside Factors Uncontrollable:

Outside variables could impact some unanticipated difficulties beyond the homesteading community's control. This might include changes in government policy, harsh weather, or the world economy. Resilience, flexibility, and, in some situations, lobbying efforts are necessary to navigate obstacles impacted by outside forces.

Managing Both Immediate and Extended Reactions:

While handling unanticipated obstacles, balancing short- and long-term solutions becomes difficult. In addition to considering the long-term sustainability of their answers, homesteaders must take rapid action when required to solve pressing concerns. Finding the ideal balance guarantees immediate actions complement the community's long-term objectives.

❖ **Transformative Facets of Overcoming Unexpected Obstacles:**

Enhanced Adaptability

The ability to overcome unanticipated obstacles strengthens the homesteading community's resilience. Overcoming unforeseen obstacles and coming out on top fosters a group resilience that can endure further difficulties. The community's enhanced ability to adapt and flourish amid uncertainty indicates its transformational quality.

Creativity and Problem-Solving Abilities:

The growth of creativity and problem-solving abilities is a component of the transformational element. Thinking outside the box and being flexible are essential when dealing with unanticipated obstacles. A culture of creativity spreads across the community when homesteaders take an active role in solving unforeseen issues.

Unity and Cohesion in the Community:

Overcoming unanticipated obstacles promotes togetherness and camaraderie throughout the community. Community members develop close relationships via their common experience of confronting and conquering obstacles. This transforming element fosters a feeling of cohesion, reciprocal assistance, and a common dedication to the homesteading way of life.

The Growth and Learning Mindset

Homesteaders who actively address unanticipated obstacles have a development and learning mentality. Rather than seeing issues as insurmountable roadblocks, they perceive them as chances for growth and development. The community is infused with this transforming quality, which fosters a culture of ongoing learning and development.

Adjusting to Changing Situations:

The community's ability to adjust to shifting conditions is a component of the transformational element. Homesteaders who successfully navigate unanticipated obstacles acquire the abilities and perspective necessary to adjust to changing circumstances. This flexibility guarantees the community's long-term viability and prosperity.

In summary, overcoming unanticipated obstacles is an essential part of the homesteading way of life. The dynamic aspect of homesteading, the development of adaptation and resilience, the avoidance of escalation, and the ongoing learning and development of the community make it significant. Proactive planning, cooperative problem-solving, flexibility, adaptability, and learning from mistakes serve as guiding principles for the methodologies, which include emergency preparedness plans, risk assessment and mitigation, community training sessions, information-sharing networks, and crisis communication procedures.

Careful care must be given to issues about few resources, intricate networks of interdependent systems, psychological strain, uncontrollable outside influences, and striking a balance between immediate and long-term solutions. Some of the transforming elements are improved resilience, inventiveness and problem-solving abilities, community solidarity and togetherness, a development and learning attitude, and flexibility in the face of changing conditions. Homesteaders actively overcome unanticipated obstacles, which helps build a community that is devoted to sustainable living and is robust, adaptive, and always changing.

10.2 Navigating Legal and Zoning Issues

Although it provides a route to self-sufficient and sustainable living, homesteading has difficulties. This section delves into the importance, guiding principles, approaches, difficulties, and transformational elements of resolving legal and zoning issues in homesteading.

The Importance of Handling Legal and Zoning Concerns:

Legal Adherence and Land Utilization:

The need for legal compliance and appropriate land use underpins the relevance of managing zoning and legal difficulties in homesteading. Following local laws and zoning rules while establishing living areas, farms, and other buildings helps homesteaders ensure their operations comply with legal requirements and larger community norms.

Property Rights and Land Security:

Ensuring land security and property rights requires navigating zoning and legal obstacles. Homesteaders put a lot of time, energy, and money into making their property suitable for a sustainable life. Comprehending and abiding by legal frameworks safeguards their entitlements to use and savor their stuff without encountering legal conflicts or possible confiscation.

Respect and Community Integration:

Respect and community cohesion are fostered by legal compliance. When homesteaders abide by zoning rules and municipal ordinances, they become essential members of their communities. This integration requires building good connections with neighbors, municipal officials, and other community members who may live in the same region.

Planning for the future and sustainability:

Handling zoning and legal difficulties is essential to the long-term viability of homesteading methods. Homesteaders can prepare for the future, including possible additions or modifications to their homesteads, when they comprehend and abide by the restrictions. This foresight guarantees their legal compliance with sustainable living practices.

❖ **Guidelines for Handling Legal and Zoning Matters:**

Knowledge of Education:

Educational knowledge is one of the most important concepts in resolving legal and zoning concerns. Homesteaders must know about zoning rules, land use ordinances, and municipal legislation. This idea allows homesteaders to make wise judgments and promotes a proactive approach to legal compliance.

Cooperation with Municipalities:

A guiding concept that prioritizes cooperation and open communication is collaboration with local authorities. Homesteaders should build strong bonds with municipal authorities, zoning boards, and other organizations. This cooperative strategy guarantees legal compliance while fostering a shared knowledge of homesteading principles.

Localized Advocacy:

The idea of community advocacy pushes homesteaders to participate in local and community forums over land use regulations. Homesteaders may shape and influence local policy by attending community meetings, campaigning for rules that are favorable to homesteading, and contributing to conversations about sustainable living.

Flexibility and Adaptability:

Adaptability and flexibility are fundamental concepts for navigating legal and zoning challenges successfully. Homesteaders should be prepared to modify their plans and methods to comply with changing restrictions. In reaction to modifications in zoning regulations or other legal constraints, this idea promotes initiative.

Considering Ethics:

Ethical concerns are A guiding concept highlighting the significance of carrying out homesteading operations ethically and responsibly. Homesteaders need to respect moral principles in land usage, prioritize environmental sustainability, and consider how their actions will affect their neighbors and the community.

❖ **Strategies for Handling Legal and Zoning Concerns:**

Consultation by Lawyer:

Hiring experts knowledgeable about zoning rules and local legislation is one approach to seeking legal counsel. Homesteaders seeking to assure compliance and thoroughly grasp legal requirements should speak with zoning and land use specialists.

Research and Analysis on Zoning:

Homesteaders are required by methodology for zoning research and analysis, which entails a detailed investigation of local zoning laws. This entails awareness of the zoning classifications, approved land uses, and any limitations that could apply to certain homesteading endeavors. Homesteaders may benefit from this study by learning about the legal boundaries that surround their operations.

Engaging the Community:

Active participation in neighborhood gatherings, forums, and activities is a key component of the community engagement process. Through interacting with neighbors and local government representatives, homesteaders may form bonds, exchange personal tales, and add to conversations over zoning regulations. This interaction promotes a feeling of mutual understanding and support within the group.

Workshops on Legal Compliance:

One approach to provide homesteaders and the community at large educational opportunities is to host legal compliance seminars. Topics like zoning laws, land use policy, and best practices for legal compliance may be covered in these sessions. Workshops help to increase knowledge of legal problems and foster a shared understanding of them.

Campaign Activities:

Homesteaders actively engage in advocacy efforts to support laws favorable to homesteading. These are known as advocacy initiatives. This approach might include starting or joining advocacy organizations, appearing at public hearings, and making presentations supporting self-sufficient and sustainable living methods. Local policies are shaped in part by advocacy campaigns.

❖ **Difficulties in Handling Legal and Zoning Matters:**

Different Regulations:

Navigating legal and zoning difficulties may be difficult when rules are inconsistent. Diverse jurisdictions may have diverse zoning rules and land use restrictions, which may confuse homesteaders who can be subject to contradictory obligations. One must be flexible and thoroughly aware of local laws to overcome this obstacle.

Shifting Regulatory Environment:

It is difficult to keep up with the constantly evolving regulatory environment, particularly for homesteaders who could see changes to land use regulations or zoning rules in the future. It takes constant attention to detail and a dedication to remain educated to stay on top of regulatory developments and modify homesteading methods properly.

Opposition from Conventional Norms:

Navigating legal and zoning difficulties may be difficult when faced with resistance from old conventions. Homesteading methods can upset social norms, which elicit resistance or criticism from people or organizations that follow more traditional land usage patterns. It will need significant community participation and advocacy initiatives to overcome this obstacle.

Insufficient Legal Resources:

Homesteaders may face difficulties due to a lack of legal resources, especially those struggling financially. Retaining legal experts for advice or representation may be difficult for low-income people or communities. Acquiring reasonably priced or pro bono legal aid becomes essential in tackling this obstacle.

Misunderstandings about Zoning:

Homesteaders may face difficulties as a result of misconceptions about zoning laws. Inadvertent breaches of zoning rules may result from unclear or misinterpreted regulations. To guarantee a clear grasp of zoning laws, addressing this difficulty requires extensive study, legal consulting, and open engagement with local authorities.

❖ **Transformative Elements of Handling Zoning and Legal Concerns:**

Encouraging the Community:

The homesteading community is empowered when it navigates zoning and legal challenges. Through comprehension and involvement in legal procedures, homesteaders can argue for their way of life with authority. This transformational feature encourages a feeling of action and influence in local rules among the community members.

Legal Knowledge:

The homesteading community's growing legal literacy is one of the transforming aspects. Homesteaders learn about local laws, land use regulations, and regulatory procedures as they work through legal and zoning challenges. The community's capacity to make wise judgments and effectively represent its interests is improved by this legal literacy.

Creating Collaborative Connections:

Successfully navigating zoning and legal challenges encourages homesteaders and local government officials to develop cooperative partnerships. Establishing open channels of communication, fostering understanding, and cooperating to develop solutions that strike a balance between the needs of the community and local laws are all part of this transformational process.

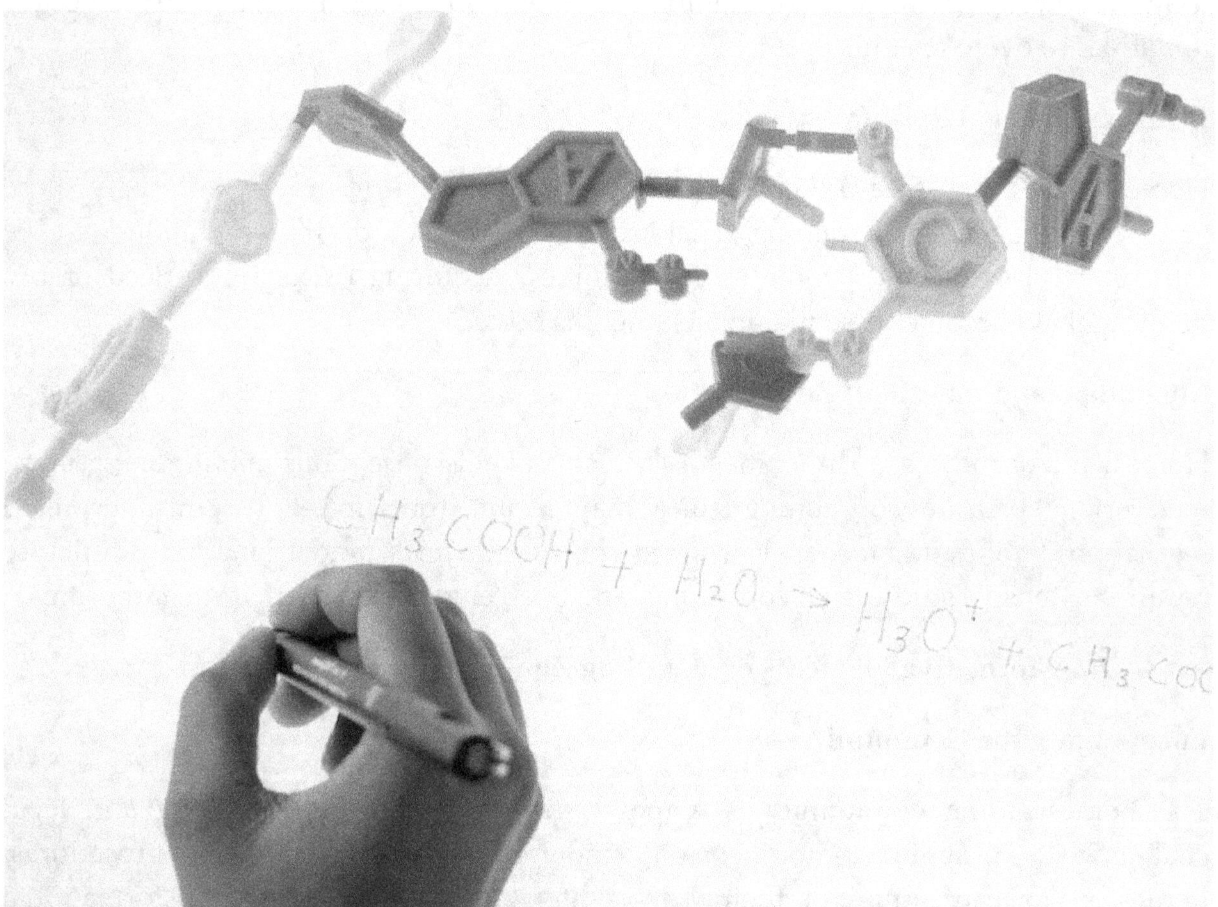

Influence on Policy and Advocacy:

Actively managing zoning and legal challenges as homesteaders helps with lobbying and policy impact. This transformational element entails homesteaders participating in debates, supporting laws that favor homesteading, and influencing the creation of laws that encourage self-sufficient and sustainable living.

Changing with the Regulations:

The community's adjustment to regulatory changes is a part of the transformational element. Homesteaders who successfully navigate zoning and legal challenges have the knowledge and perspective to adjust to changing legal environments. This flexibility guarantees the community's long-term viability and resistance to shifting laws.

In summary, resolving legal and zoning conflicts is crucial to living on a homestead. Legal observance, land security, community integration, and sustainability planning are important. The approaches include legal consulting, zoning research and analysis, community participation, legal compliance seminars, and advocacy activities. The values of educational awareness, partnership with local authorities, community advocacy, flexibility, and ethical concerns underpin them.

Consideration must be given to issues with inconsistent rules, shifting regulatory environments, opposition from conventional standards, a lack of legal resources, and misinterpretations of zoning laws. Among the transforming elements are community empowerment, legal knowledge, fostering cooperative partnerships, lobbying and policy impact, and regulatory change adaption. Homesteaders actively resolve zoning and legal concerns, which helps build a resilient, empowered, and law-abiding community that upholds sustainable living ideas.

10.3 Economic Sustainability

A key component of the homesteading lifestyle is economic sustainability, which balances the need for financial stability and the desire for self-sufficiency. In the context of homesteading, we examine the importance, guiding principles, approaches, difficulties, and transformational elements of attaining economic sustainability in this section.

❖ **The Importance of a Sustainable Economy:**

Having enough money:

Achieving financial independence is the key to economic sustainability in homesteading. The goal of homesteading is to become less dependent on outside sources for necessities like food, energy, and shelter. Economic sustainability guarantees homesteaders can maintain their way of life using resources and revenue from their sources.

Extended Durability:

The long-term sustainability of homesteading activities is influenced by economic sustainability. By establishing financially sustainable methods, homesteaders strengthen their capacity to withstand adversity, make changes, and guarantee the sustainability of their independent way of life. This long-term viability is essential for homesteading communities to be resilient and stable.

Allocation of Resources and Efficiency:

Efficient use and distribution of resources are necessary for economic sustainability. To optimize their operational efficiency, homesteaders must prudently manage their financial resources by balancing their revenue and costs. This guarantees the prudent use of resources, promoting the sustainability of activities like infrastructure development, energy generation, and agriculture.

Collective Welfare:

The general well-being of the homesteading community is influenced by each homestead's capacity to maintain a sustainable economy. A financially secure homestead may help build a strong and vibrant homesteading community by actively supporting local projects, participating in group activities, and so on. This connectivity emphasizes how important economic sustainability is on a larger scale.

❖ **Economic Sustainability Principles:**

Stream Diversification of Income:

Diversification of revenue sources is a fundamental tenet of sustainable economies. Homesteaders should look into various revenue-generating opportunities, such as selling crops, holding workshops, rendering services, or producing goods with additional value. Diversification improves financial stability by lowering dependence on a single source of income.

Ability to Adjust to Market Trends:

A guiding concept that stresses being abreast of customer tastes, market needs, and economic changes is adaptability to market trends. Homesteaders must exhibit flexibility in adapting their offerings to suit changing market conditions. This flexibility guarantees the preservation of economic viability amidst changing patterns.

Effective Resource Administration:

The concept of efficient resource management is making the best use of all available resources, such as labor, materials, and time. It is recommended that homesteaders adopt techniques that reduce waste, enhance efficiency, and optimize their homesteading endeavors. Economic sustainability is supported by effective resource management since it lowers costs and raises yields.

Infrastructure Investment:

One guiding concept that emphasizes the significance of strategic investments to improve economic sustainability is infrastructure investment. This might be creating systems that use less energy, managing water better, or creating buildings that can accommodate a variety of homesteading activities. Thoughtful infrastructure investments enhance long-term financial resilience.

Benefit-Cost Analysis:

Homesteaders are encouraged to evaluate the financial sustainability of their operations by using the cost-benefit analysis approach. Analyzing practices in-depth helps determine which ones provide the best returns on investment and contribute to economic sustainability. Frequent assessments guarantee that monetary resources are assigned to endeavors that provide the most significant influence.

❖ **Approaches to Financial Sustainability:**

Development of Small-Scale Businesses:

One approach to small-scale company growth is starting and expanding homestead companies. Some examples include selling extra food, handcrafted goods, or services like workshops or training sessions. Growing small enterprises promotes economic sustainability and brings in extra revenue.

Market Analysis and Customer Involvement:

Homesteaders may remain current on customer preferences and market developments by interacting with consumers and doing market research. Homesteaders may improve economic sustainability by meeting market expectations by customizing their goods and services to their target audience's needs.

Resource-Conscious Methods:

Implementing resource-efficient practices is centered on waste reduction and resource optimization. This might include using sustainable practices like permaculture, effective water management, or renewable energy sources. Resource-efficient methods save expenses and promote economic sustainability in addition to environmental sustainability.

Planning and Budgeting for Finances:

Budgeting and financial planning are examples of approaches that include strategic financial resource management. Homesteaders need to watch spending, make reasonable budgets, and make investment plans for the future. This systematic approach to financial management promotes economic sustainability by ensuring that resources are distributed effectively.

Initial Requirements for Capital:

Homesteaders may have difficulty obtaining the initial funding to launch or grow their businesses. Making large upfront expenditures for infrastructure investments, purchasing equipment, or switching to new procedures may be essential. This difficulty may be addressed by looking for community support or by coming up with innovative financial options.

Restricted Market Access:

Economic sustainability may be hampered by limited market access, particularly for homesteaders in isolated or distant areas. To overcome this obstacle, one option is to look into other distribution methods, create online platforms, or participate in neighborhood farmers' markets to increase market accessibility.

Seasonal Changes in Income:

Homesteaders who depend on agriculture or other seasonal occupations have the difficulty of unpredictable seasonal revenue. An uneven annual income may make financial planning and budgeting difficult. This problem can be solved by putting tactics like value-added product development or off-season revenue sources into practice.

Against Conventional Agriculture in Competition:

The wider market is a problem for homesteaders because of competition from conventional agriculture. Large-scale farming businesses could be more profitable and have a stronger market presence. To successfully compete, homesteaders must stress the distinctive features of their sustainable practices, concentrate on specialized markets, and distinguish their goods.

❖ **Aspects of Economic Sustainability That Are Transformative:**

Adaptable Community Economy

Building a resilient community economy is facilitated by achieving economic sustainability. The revolutionary component is building a network of financially secure homesteads that mutually support one another — the homesteading community benefits from this resilience, which promotes stability and strength in the economy.

Inventiveness and Flexibility:

Within the community of homesteaders, economic viability encourages creativity and flexibility. Homesteaders actively look for novel ways to solve financial problems, try out novel techniques, and adjust to shifting market dynamics. This transformational element creates a community that values resilience and ongoing progress.

Diversification of sources of income and skills:

The search for economic sustainability gives rise to a transformational aspect: the diversification of talents and revenue sources. Homesteaders experiment with various revenue-generating ventures and acquire a wide range of skills. This diversification lessens the community's reliance on a single revenue source and increases its overall resiliency.

Community Assistance and Cooperation:

Collaborative and supportive communities are fostered by economic sustainability. The transformational element is when homesteaders band together to exchange resources, work together on projects, and solve problems related to the economy as a group. Individual homesteads' prosperity and general well-being are improved by this feeling of communal support.

Identity-based on culture and economy:

Creating a unique cultural and economic identity for the homesteading community is a component of the transformational element. Homesteaders may create a distinctive identity for themselves that is based on environmental care, self-sufficiency, and a dedication to sustainable living, thanks to economic sustainability. For the community, this identity becomes a source of resilience and pride.

In summary, attaining economic sustainability is a key component of the homesteading lifestyle. Long-term sustainability, effective resource management, financial independence, and communal well-being are important. Methodologies include small-scale business development, market research and consumer engagement, resource-efficient practices, financial planning and budgeting, and collaborative ventures.

These are guided by principles of diversification of income streams, adaptability to market trends, efficient resource management, investment in infrastructure, and cost-benefit analysis. Careful care must be given to market volatility, starting capital needs, market accessibility issues, erratic seasonal revenue, and competition from traditional agriculture. A robust community economy, creativity and adaptation, diversity of skill sets and sources of income, community support and cooperation, and the creation of a unique cultural and economic identity are some of the transforming elements. Homesteaders actively work for economic sustainability, which helps to build a strong, self-sufficient, and culturally diverse community devoted to sustainable living practices.

Aspect	Explanation
Significance of Economic Sustainability	Achieving financial independence, ensuring long-term viability, efficient resource allocation, and contributing to community well-being.
Principles of Economic Sustainability	Diversification of income streams, adaptability to market trends, efficient resource management, investment in infrastructure, and cost-benefit analysis.
Methodologies for Economic Sustainability	Small-scale business development, market research, resource-efficient practices, financial planning, and collaborative ventures.
Challenges of Economic Sustainability	Market volatility, initial capital requirements, limited access to markets, seasonal income variability, and competition with conventional agriculture.
Transformative Aspects of Economic Sustainability	Building a resilient community economy, fostering innovation and adaptability, diversification of skills and income streams, community support, and collaboration, and developing a distinct cultural and economic identity.
Conclusion	Economic sustainability is fundamental for financial independence, long-term viability, and community well-being in homesteading. Guided by principles and methodologies, challenges require thoughtful consideration, and transformative aspects contribute to a resilient and culturally rich homesteading community committed to sustainable living.

10.4 Adapting to Climate Change

As the effects of a changing climate become more apparent, homesteaders must prioritize adapting to these changes. This section explores the importance, guiding principles, approaches, obstacles, and transformational elements of climate change adaptation in the context of homesteading.

❖ **The Importance of Climate Change Adaptation:**

Ecological Guardianship:

Environmental care is the key to homesteading's adaptation to climate change. Homesteaders understand their responsibility to preserve and maintain the environment since they are often closely bonded to the land. As a proactive reaction to the problems brought on by a warming globe, adapting to climate change shows a dedication to sustainable living methods and appropriate land management.

Sustainability and Resilience:

Changing with the times improves homesteading methods' sustainability and resilience. Homesteaders must modify their farming practices, water management plans, and general homestead architecture to meet the difficulties posed by changing climate patterns and increasing the frequency of severe weather events. Developing resilience makes homesteading initiatives sustainable over the long run.

Maintaining Biodiversity

Ecosystems may be upset by climate change, endangering biodiversity. Homesteaders are essential to preserving biodiversity because they modify their lifestyles to benefit the native plants and animals. This might include developing habitats for animals, planting native species, and putting in place sustainable land use techniques that reduce adverse effects on the nearby environment.

Collective Welfare:

The capacity of the homesteading community to adjust to climate change is intimately related to its well-being. Extreme weather events may all impact food production, water availability, general living circumstances, precipitation patterns, and growing season changes. Homesteaders strengthen their community's resilience and well-being by adjusting to climate change.

❖ **Climate Change Adaptation Principles:**

Keeping an Eye on Things:

Constant observation and monitoring is a cornerstone of climate change adaptation. Homesteaders must constantly monitor the seasonal variations in temperature, precipitation, and the frequency of severe weather occurrences in their area. This concept highlights how important it is to be aware of the unique climatic problems of the homesteading site.

Adaptability and Flexibility:

Flexibility and adaptability guiding concepts highlight the need to modify procedures in response to shifting climatic circumstances. In response to noted changes in the climate, homesteaders should be prepared to adjust their planting dates, water management strategies, and other practices. This idea promotes a proactive and flexible strategy for adjusting to climate change.

Practices for Regeneration:

Regenerative techniques are based on ideas that prioritize improving and restoring the land's health. This entails using agroforestry practices, cultivating cover crops, and enhancing soil health. Homesteaders may help with climate adaptation using regenerative methods because they create resilient ecosystems that resist environmental pressures.

Water Management and Conservation:

Water management and conservation are essential concepts. Changes in precipitation patterns brought about by climate change often result in droughts or periods of higher rainfall. To guarantee a consistent and sustainable water supply for their homesteading endeavors, homesteaders had to use water conservation techniques like rainwater gathering and effective irrigation.

Sequestration of Carbon:

One idea highlighting homesteaders' role in reducing climate change is carbon sequestration. Tree planting, cover crops, and no-till farming help sequester carbon and reduce greenhouse gas emissions. This idea supports the more general objective of lowering the carbon footprint of the homestead.

❖ **Approaches to Climate Change Adaptation:**

Climate-Sensitive Farming:

Implementing climate-resilient agricultural practices aims to improve crop choices, planting dates, and farming methods to resist the difficulties climate change brings. To improve total farm resilience, this may include selecting drought-resistant crops, varying crop kinds, and using agro ecological concepts.

Systems for Harvesting and Managing Water:

One approach to addressing shifting precipitation patterns is developing water collection and management technologies. To secure a consistent water supply during dry spells or sporadic rainfall, homesteaders may install rainwater collection systems, build catchment basins, and invest in effective irrigation techniques.

Design of Permaculture:

Permaculture design is an approach that incorporates resilience, biodiversity, and sustainability. Homesteaders may establish self-sustaining ecosystems that resemble natural patterns by using permaculture principles. Permaculture design promotes climate adaptation by improving the homestead environment's overall resilience.

Building Soil and Preserving It:

Building and preserving soil health is an approach that recognizes the pivotal function of soil in adapting to climate change. Composting, cover crops, and limited tillage are a few techniques that improve the fertility and structure of soil. Healthy soils provide a strong basis for sustainable agriculture methods and are more resistant to adverse weather occurrences.

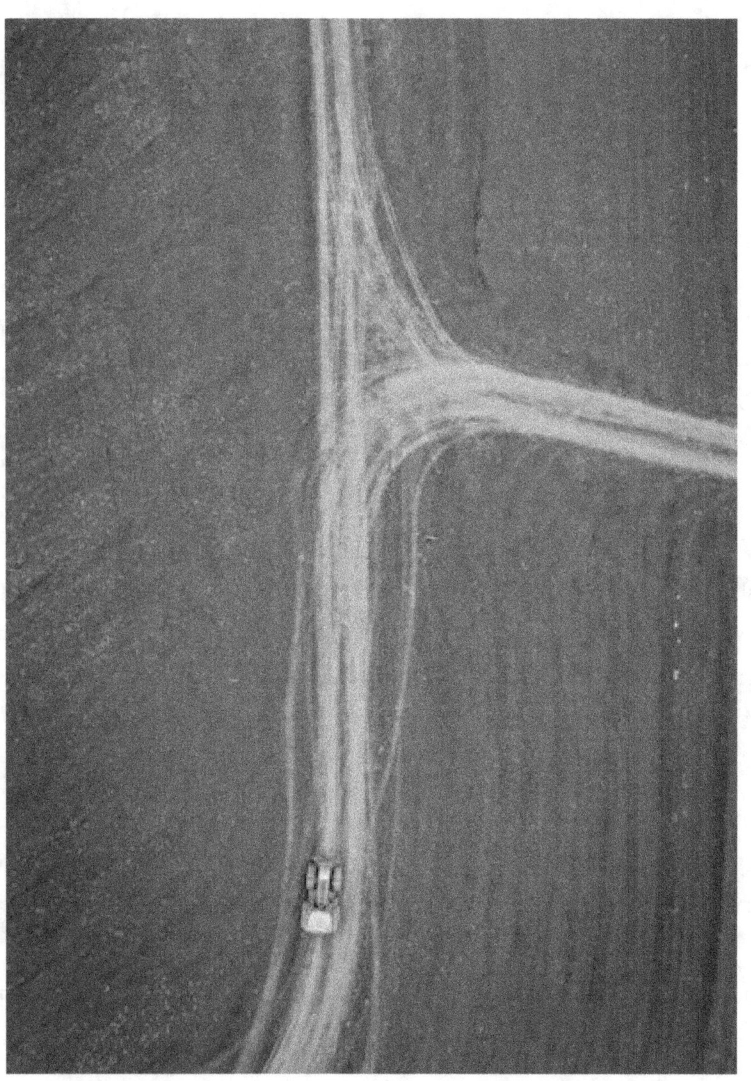

Renewable Energy and Energy Efficiency:

One strategy for lowering the carbon footprint of homesteading operations is to promote energy efficiency and use renewable energy sources. This entails reducing dependency on fossil fuels, using solar or wind energy, and implementing energy-efficient devices. The overarching objective of minimizing climate change is in line with the use of renewable energy techniques.

❖ **Difficulties in Climate Change Adaptation:**

Erratic patterns of weather

It is difficult to adapt to climate change because of the erratic weather. Unexpected frosts, heat waves, and storms are extreme weather that may affect household planning and disturb agricultural cycles. Effective adaptation requires the development of coping mechanisms for unpredictable weather.

Restrictions on Resources:

Implementing solutions for climate adaptation may face obstacles due to limited resources, such as restricted financial resources and limited access to technology. It could be hard for homesteaders to get the necessary equipment or upgrade their infrastructure to make it more climate resilient. Resource constraints must be overcome with innovative ideas and community support.

Pests and Species Migration:

Local ecosystems may be impacted by changes in plant and animal species distribution brought on by climate change. For homesteaders, the spread of pests and the influx of new species might provide difficulties. Vigilance, observation, and the creation of sustainable pest control plans are necessary to adjust to these changes.

Policies and Rules Governing Land Use:

Current land use laws and policies don't always consider climate adaptation. Regulations restricting specific practices—like agroforestry or water harvesting—may make it difficult for homesteaders to implement them. Engagement with local authorities and advocacy for climate-friendly legislation is essential to overcome this obstacle.

Education and Awareness of the Community:

Education and community awareness are key components of effectiveness in adapting to climate change. Homesteaders may find it difficult to convince the larger community of the value of climate adaptation. Developing a shared awareness of the effects of climate change, encouraging open communication, and implementing educational programs are necessary to overcome this obstacle.

❖ **The Changing Face of Climate Change Adaptation:**

Restoring the Environment:

Climate change adaptation promotes ecological restoration as a transformational feature. Homesteaders actively participate in activities that improve the general health of the land by regenerating and restoring ecosystems. Committing to leaving the land in better ecological shape for future generations is a key component of this transformational feature.

Community Involvement:

As a transformational factor, climate adaptation promotes communal cooperation. Homesteaders actively cooperate to solve climate concerns because they understand how their actions are interrelated. This cooperative strategy improves information exchange, fortifies community ties, and builds a support network for addressing climate-related concerns.

Novel Approaches to Sustainable Practices:

Sustainable practice innovation is a part of the transformational component. Homesteaders are motivated to investigate and use creative solutions that conform to sustainable principles by the need to adapt to climate change. This might include implementing cutting-edge technology for climate adaptation, creating climate-resilient infrastructure, or testing out novel crop types.

Adaptable Food Systems:

As a transformational element, climate change adaptation aids in the creation of resilient food systems. Homesteading aims to build resilient and diversified food systems that can endure the effects of climatic unpredictability. This entails moving toward crops suited to the local environment, sustainable farming methods, and methods for preserving food.

Change in Culture in Favor of Sustainability:

The transformational element encompasses a movement in culture toward sustainability. The homesteading community instills the cultural value of adapting to climate change. This change in culture includes a strong understanding of how human activity affects the environment and a dedication to sustainable and ethical living.

In summary, the homesteading lifestyle necessitates climate change adaptation due to the importance of resilience, biodiversity preservation, environmental stewardship, and communal well-being. Methodologies such as climate-resilient agriculture, water harvesting systems, permaculture design, soil building, and energy efficiency are guided by observation and monitoring, adaptability, regenerative practices, water conservation, and carbon sequestration. Erratic weather patterns, scarce resources, migratory animals, land use regulations, and public awareness must be considered.

Some of the transforming elements include ecological restoration, community cooperation, sustainable practice innovation, resilient food systems, and a movement in culture toward sustainability. Homesteaders actively participate in climate change adaptation, which helps build resilient, sustainable, and culturally diverse communities dedicated to reducing climate change's effects.

10.5 Learning from Setbacks: Case Studies of Successful Homesteaders

Setbacks are a part of the homesteading path and must be learned from them to create a resilient and prosperous farm. This section examines, via case studies of successful homesteaders, the importance, tenets, approaches, difficulties, and transforming elements of learning from failures.

❖ **The Importance of Gaining Knowledge from Failures:**

Adaptivity and Resilience:

In homesteading, learning from failures resides in developing resilience and adaptation. Whatever the cause, setbacks—crop failures, unforeseen weather occurrences, or infrastructural issues—offer homesteaders invaluable chances to modify their methods, develop their problem-solving abilities, and strengthen their homestead against future difficulties. For long-term success, this adaptive resilience is essential.

Constant Enhancement:

A dedication to ongoing development is inextricably linked with the ability to learn from mistakes. Successful homesteaders see obstacles as opportunities for improvement rather than as failure indicators. Every setback is an opportunity to review, hone tactics, and implement enhancements. This commitment to ongoing development helps the homestead remain successful and sustainable overall.

Information Exchange and Establishing Communities:

Setbacks provide the homesteading community a forum for information exchange and community development. Homesteaders who encounter failure and grow from it often impart their knowledge, insights, and fixes to others. The homesteading community is strengthened by this culture of sharing information, which creates a helpful network where people may benefit from the collective expertise obtained from overcoming obstacles.

Alignment of Goals and Vision:

Homesteaders may realign their vision and aims with the reality of their surroundings by learning from their failures. Homesteaders often reevaluate their long-term intentions in response to setbacks, modifying their objectives in light of real-world experiences. Maintaining a clear vision and purpose in facing difficulties depends on this alignment.

❖ **Guidelines for Recovering from Failures:**

Contemplation and Evaluation:

Thinking and analyzing things is a fundamental part of learning from failures. Prosperous homesteaders contemplate the elements causing obstacles, examine the underlying reasons, and comprehend the consequences. The foundation for well-informed decision-making and tactical modifications is laid by this reflecting process.

Flexibility and Adaptation:

The guiding concepts of adaptation and flexibility highlight the capacity to modify plans in response to obstacles. Those homesteaders who can overcome obstacles are those who are flexible. This might include adapting new methods in response to difficulties, altering construction plans, or switching crop kinds.

Adding Variability:

The idea of diversification encourages people to take a broad and multidimensional approach. One typically realizes after suffering disappointments that a varied farmstead is more resilient to adversity. Crop choices, revenue sources, and even the development of substitute techniques for obtaining water and energy are examples of diversification.

Developing Resilience:

Learning from setbacks is directly related to the guiding idea of building resilience. Profitable homesteaders actively work to improve their homesteads' resilience by taking lessons from prior failures. This might include investing in risk-reduction techniques, creating robust plants, or improving infrastructure.

Learning and the Development of Skills:

In the face of failure, education and skill development are fundamental values. A learning mentality encourages homesteaders to seek information proactively, learn new skills, and keep up with industry best practices. This lifelong learning dedication ensures that failures turn into worthwhile teaching moments rather than insurmountable roadblocks.

❖ **Techniques for Acquiring Knowledge from Failures:**

Analyses and Case Studies:

One approach that gives homesteaders concrete examples of overcoming obstacles is to analyze case studies of failures. People may learn useful tips, possible hazards to avoid, and techniques for overcoming failures by reading about the experiences of other homesteaders.

Constant Observation and Assessment:

Assessing homestead habits, performance, and results regularly is part of continuous monitoring and evaluation. Homesteaders who take lessons from their failures proactively monitor their activities, spot potential problem areas, and make necessary adjustments. This process guarantees a flexible and adaptable homesteading strategy.

Networking and Involvement in the Community:

One approach that promotes shared learning is interacting with the homesteading community and networking with colleagues. Attending courses, online forums, or local homesteading organizations allows people to share experiences, learn from each other's failures, and access a wealth of collective knowledge that helps them overcome obstacles.

Mentoring and advising:

Seeking mentoring and assistance is a learning-acceleration tactic. Wealthy homesteaders often credit their resiliency to the advice of mentors who have experienced comparable hardships. A great way to learn from other people's experiences and get useful ideas on conquering obstacles is via mentoring.

Inventiveness and Trials:

Trying new methods and technologies is a process that is part of innovation and experimentation. Homesteaders who are prepared to try new things and are open to innovation are those who learn from their mistakes. This might include experimenting with various crop kinds, investigating environmentally friendly technology, or coming up with original ways to deal with obstacles.

❖ **Difficulties in Learning from Failures:**

Emotional Hardiness:

Emotional resilience is one of the difficulties in learning from failures. Overcoming setbacks demands a resilient and upbeat outlook since they may be emotionally draining. Successful homesteaders always face the difficulty of navigating the emotional implications of failures.

Restrictions on Resources:

Learning may be hampered by time and money limits, among other resource limitations. It might take more resources to implement improvements or modifications in response to setbacks. Successful homesteaders must ingeniously navigate resource limitations, and they must discover effective methods to put their learning to use.

Breaking Habitual Behaviors:

It could be difficult for homesteaders to break bad habits that lead to failures. One must be open to adapting to break free from established or customary practices. One must question accepted wisdom and modify methods to get desired results to learn from failures effectively.

Harmonizing Innovation with Tradition:

Adapting from setbacks is a problem homesteaders encounter as they balance tradition and innovation. Although there is merit to established methods, innovation must be welcomed to remain flexible. Careful thought must be given to finding the ideal balance between tried-and-true techniques and cutting-edge alternatives.

Successful Interaction:

It may be difficult to communicate failure lessons effectively, particularly in a community. To ensure that the information they have acquired is properly shared, homesteaders must figure out how to openly and honestly communicate their experiences. Problems with communication may impede the process of group learning.

❖ **The Transformational Potential of Learning from Failures:**

Developing an Attitude of Growth:

A growth mindset is cultivated as a transforming element by learning from failures. Successful homesteaders see obstacles as chances for improvement rather than signs of failure. This mentality change encourages optimism, fortitude in adversity, and a persistent dedication to growth and learning.

Community Adaptability:

The transformational element encompasses resilience throughout the community — the homesteading community benefits from a shared experience when failures are learned from. When a community actively learns from its failures, everyone in the group adds to its strength and flexibility, creating collective resilience.

Inventiveness and Flexibility:

Resilience fosters invention and adaptability, which are transformational qualities. A culture of innovation is embraced by prosperous homesteaders, who always look for better ways to solve problems and change their methods in light of new knowledge. This transforming element adds to the homesteading techniques' overall vitality and sustainability.

Self-reliance and Empowerment:

The transforming element encompasses self-reliance and empowerment. Homesteaders who learn from their failures are more equipped to face obstacles independently. This feeling of independence transforms, creating a group of people who can overcome obstacles with courage and creativity.

Building a Community of Learning:

A transforming feature of learning from failures is how a learning community is developed. By actively sharing their knowledge, ideas, and solutions, homesteaders foster a culture of lifelong learning. This transforming feature ensures that failures become group learning experiences that build a strong and capable homesteading community.

In summary, one essential and transforming part of the homesteading experience is learning from failures. The importance is in strengthening resilience, encouraging ongoing development, disseminating information among community members, and coordinating objectives with real-world experiences. Challenges include emotional resilience, resource constraints, overcoming habitual practices, balancing tradition and innovation, and effective communication. Principles of reflection, adaptation, diversification, resilience building, education, and methodologies like case studies, continuous monitoring, networking, mentorship, and innovation guide all of these.

A growth mentality, community resilience, creativity and adaptability, empowerment and self-reliance, and the development of a learning community are some of the transforming elements. Homesteaders help build resilient, adaptable, and empowered communities devoted to the ideals of sustainable living when they welcome setbacks as chances for development and learning.

Conclusion

With a great feeling of achievement and a common vision for a better, more purposeful future, we close the book on "Homesteading Unplugged: An Ultimate Guide for Sustainable Living in a Digital World." We have traversed the complex web of homesteading via the chapters in this book, tying together the strands of independence, environmental awareness, and a return to the basic sources of life.

Within these pages, we have examined the wonders of raising your own food, experienced the transforming potential of sustainable practices, and learned about the deep feeling of satisfaction that comes from living peacefully with the earth. This book aims to serve as your guide on the path to more intentional and socially conscious living, covering everything from growing cattle to gardening advice to sustainable energy options.

It's more important than ever to disconnect in this day of digital dominance. "Homesteading Unplugged" strikes a healthy balance between the wisdom of traditional life and contemporary comforts, rather than dismissing technology outright. It's an appeal to take back control of our lives and create a sustainable sanctuary that benefits the environment as well as the spirit.

As we close these pages, may this ending serve as a springboard for your own homesteading journey. I hope that the inspiration seeds sown here will grow into a resilient, creative, and respectful garden of the Earth. May your homestead serve as a symbol of the potential for thoughtful cohabitation with the land in this rapidly changing digital world inside the fabric of sustainable living.

Recall that the path to sustainability is continuous and that every deliberate action you take advances the worldwide movement toward a future that is more resilient, balanced, and linked. I hope that your farm serves as a source of inspiration and a real example of the life-changing potential of adopting a sustainable, unplugged lifestyle.